RENATO MENDES CURTO JÚNIOR
- Bacharel em Letras – Português e Inglês
- Especialista em Gestão e Docência
- Diplomado em proficiência pela *Michigan University* e pela *Indiana University* – Toefl

MARIANA CARDIERI MENDONÇA
- Professora de inglês da rede particular de ensino
- Diplomada com *First Certificate in English*, pela Cambridge e pelo Toefl

INGLÊS

7

1ª edição
São Paulo, 2018

Dados Internacionais de Catalogação na Publicação (CIP)
(Câmara Brasileira do Livro, SP, Brasil)

Curto Júnior, Renato Mendes
    Apoema: inglês 7 / Renato Mendes Curto Júnior, Mariana Cardieri Mendonça. – 1. ed. – São Paulo: Editora do Brasil, 2018. – (Coleção apoema)

    ISBN 978-85-10-06952-6 (aluno)
    ISBN 978-85-10-06953-3 (professor)

    1. Inglês (Ensino fundamental) I. Mendonça, Mariana Cardieri. II. Título. III. Série.

18-20641   CDD-372.652

Índices para catálogo sistemático:
1. Inglês: Ensino fundamental 372.652
Maria Alice Ferreira – Bibliotecária – CRB-8/7964

1ª edição / 6ª impressão, 2024
Impresso na Forma Certa Gráfica Digital

Avenida das Nações Unidas, 12901
Torre Oeste, 20º andar
São Paulo, SP – CEP: 04578-910
Fone: +55 11 3226-0211
www.editoradobrasil.com.br

© Editora do Brasil S.A., 2018
Todos os direitos reservados

Direção-geral: Vicente Tortamano Avanso

Direção editorial: Felipe Ramos Poleti
Gerência editorial: Erika Caldin
Supervisão de arte e editoração: Cida Alves
Supervisão de revisão: Dora Helena Feres
Supervisão de iconografia: Léo Burgos
Supervisão de Digital: Ethel Shuña Queiroz
Supervisão de controle de processos editoriais: Marta Dias Portero
Supervisão de direitos autorais: Marilisa Bertolone Mendes

Supervisão editorial: Carla Felix Lopes
Edição: Amanda Leal e Monika Kratzer
Assistência editorial: Ana Okada e Juliana Pavoni
Auxiliar editorial: Beatriz Villanueva
Coordenação de revisão: Otacilio Palareti
Copidesque: Evelyn Zaidam Porting e Ricardo Liberal
Revisão: Alexandra Resende e Beatriz Moreira Guedes
Pesquisa iconográfica: Isabela Menezes
Assistência de arte: Samira de Souza
Design gráfico: Anexo Produção Editorial
Capa: Megalo Design
Ilustrações: Anderson Sanchez, Cristiane Viana, Daniel Klein, Danillo Souza, Dawidson França, Estúdio Ornitorrinco, João P. Mazzoco, Jótah, Kau Bispo, Leonardo Conceição, Luis Moura, Luiz Lentini, Marcelo Azalim, Marcos de Mello, Marcos Guilherme, Mario Pita e Wasteresley Lima
Coordenação de editoração eletrônica: Abdonildo José de Lima Santos
Editoração eletrônica: Daniel Campos Souza, José Anderson Campos, Flávia Jaconis, Gilvan Alves da Silva, Maira Spilack e Sérgio Rocha
Licenciamentos de textos: Cinthya Utiyama, Jennifer Xavier, Paula Harue Tozaki e Renata Garbellini
Produção fonográfica: Jennifer Xavier e Cinthya Utiyama
Controle de processos editoriais: Bruna Alves, Carlos Nunes, Jefferson Galdino, Rafael Machado e Stephanie Paparella

CONTEÚDO DIGITAL PARA ALUNOS
Cadastre-se e transforme seus estudos em uma experiência única de aprendizado:

Entre na página de cadastro:
https://sistemas.editoradobrasil.com.br/cadastro

Além dos seus dados pessoais e dos dados de sua escola, adicione ao cadastro o código do aluno, que garantirá a exclusividade do seu ingresso à plataforma.

5158667A5366808

Depois, acesse:
https://leb.editoradobrasil.com.br/
e navegue pelos conteúdos digitais de sua coleção **:D**

Lembre-se de que esse código, pessoal e intransferível, é valido por um ano. Guarde-o com cuidado, pois é a única maneira de você acessar os conteúdos da plataforma.

HEY, STUDENT! WELCOME TO APOEMA!

A língua inglesa está cada vez mais presente nos nossos dias, seja na internet, na escola ou no trabalho. Tiramos *selfies* para postar nas redes sociais, levamos o *dog* para passear e fazemos a *homework* da escola, assistimos aos nossos *youtubers* favoritos, vemos nossas séries e ouvimos nossas músicas em plataformas de *streaming* entre tantas outras coisas.

O conhecimento desta língua estrangeira é essencial para que possamos conhecer novos mundos, ampliar nossos horizontes e estarmos conectados com o que acontece ao nosso redor e no mundo. Por isso, é importante, e também gratificante, conhecer essa língua que conecta o mundo todo, compreender as culturas das quais ela faz parte.

Pensando nisso, nesta nova versão do **Apoema**, palavra da língua tupi que significa "aquele que vê mais longe", nosso objetivo não é apenas ensinar a língua estrangeira, mas também apresentar os diferentes lugares e culturas em que o inglês é o idioma nativo.

Nossa proposta é apresentar a língua inglesa de forma dinâmica, atual, interessante e ligada ao mundo real para que você possa usá-la para se comunicar, entendê-lo e escrevê-lo de forma fluente, interagindo com o mundo e expandindo seus horizontes, ou seja, vendo mais longe.

LET'S GET DOWN TO WORK!

Rawpixel.com/Shutterstock.com

SUMÁRIO

Unit 1 – How much is it?

Chapter 1	**Let's practice** – Clothing items	8
	Let's listen n' speak – Clothing items	9 e 10
Chapter 2	**Language piece** – Demonstrative pronouns	11
	– How much – interrogative form	12
	Let's listen n' speak – Shopping	13
	Vocabulary hint – Numbers	14
Chapter 3	**Let's read n' write** – Tale: The Emperor's New Suit	15 a 17
Chapter 4	**Citizenship moment** – In pictures: traditional dress around the world	18
	Project – Brazilian Traditional Attire	19

Unit 2 – Would you like some food?

Chapter 1	**Let's practice** – Food and drink items	22 e 23
	Let's listen n' speak – Grocery list	24
Chapter 2	**Language piece** – Countable and uncountable nouns	25
	– Quantifiers	26
	Let's listen n' speak – Invitations × Excuses	27
	Vocabulary hint – Modal verb can	28
Chapter 3	**Let's read n' write** – Recipe: Quinoa and Avocado Salad	29 a 31
	Project – How about writing a Class Recipe Book?	31
Chapter 4	**Tying in** – Eating Habits comic strip	32
	Project – Nutritional facts	33

Review	34 e 35
Do not forget!	36
Overcoming challenges	37

Unit 3 – Can you do this?

Chapter 1	**Let's practice** – Personal abilities	40 e 41
	Let's listen n' speak – People's skills	42
Chapter 2	**Language piece** – Modal verb can	43 e 44
	– Modal verb should	45
	Vocabulary hint – Modal verb should	45
	Let's listen n' speak – Schedule	46
Chapter 3	**Let's read n' write** – Comic strip: abilities and skills	47 a 49
Chapter 4	**Citizenship moment** – The Types of Intelligence	50
	Project – Class Types of Intelligence Pie Chart	51

Unit 4 – Where is it?

Chapter 1	**Let's practice** – Places in town	54 a 55
	Language piece – There is × There are	55
	Let's listen n' speak – Places in town	56
Chapter 2	**Let's practice** – Prepositions of place	57 e 59
	Language piece – Prepositions of place	57
	Vocabulary hint – Giving directions	59
	Let's listen n' speak – Places in the neighborhood	60
Chapter 3	**Let's read n' write** – City map	61 a 63
Chapter 4	**Tying in** – Your way under the ground	64
	Project – Brazilian Subway System	65

Review	66 e 67
Do not forget!	68
Overcoming challenges	69

Unit 5 – Did you read these stories?

Chapter 1	**Let's practice** – Book genres	72
	Language piece – Simple past (to be)	73
	Let's listen n' speak – The Expeditioners	74
Chapter 2	**Language piece** – Simple past: regular verbs	76 e 77
	Let's listen n' speak – What did you do yesterday?	78
Chapter 3	**Let's read n' write** – Gulliver's Travels	79 a 81
Chapter 4	**Citizenship moment** – International Literacy Day	82
	Project – Fight Illiteracy	83

Unit 6 – Did you see this movie?

Chapter 1	**Let's practice** – Movie genres	86
	– Music genres	87
	– Musical instruments	87
	Let's listen n' speak – Movie on exhibition	88
Chapter 2	**Language piece** – Simple past: irregular verbs	90
	Vocabulary hint – Vowel sounds	91
	Let's listen n' speak – I saw a nice movie yesterday	92
Chapter 3	**Let's read n' write** – Movie review	93 a 95
Chapter 4	**Tying in** – Playing for change	96
	Project – Brazilian Popular Songs	97

Review	98 e 99
Do not forget!	100
Overcoming challenges	101

Unit 7 – What do they look like?

Chapter 1	**Let's practice** – Describing people	104 e 105
	Let's listen n' speak – Describing people	106
Chapter 2	**Language piece** – Describing people	107 e 108
	Let's listen n' speak – Describing people – part II	109
	Language piece – Used to	110
	Vocabulary hint – Used to	110
Chapter 3	**Let's read n' write** – Movie character's profile	111 a 113
Chapter 4	**Citizenship moment** – The Universal Declaration of Human Rights	114
	Project – Human Rights	115

Unit 8 – What is the weather like?

Chapter 1	**Let's practice** – Weather and climate	118 e 119
	Let's listen n' speak – Grover forecast	120
Chapter 2	**Language piece** – Past continuous	121 a 123
	Vocabulary hint – The /-ng/ sound	123
	Let's listen n' speak – What was happening yesterday?	124
Chapter 3	**Let's read n' write** – Weather forecast	125 a 127
Chapter 4	**Tying in** – Weather extremes	128
	Project – Brazilian regional climates	129

Review	130 e 131
Do not forget!	132
Overcoming challenges	133

Workbook	134 a 149
Expert's point	150 a 153
Three steps to say "no" gracefully	150 e 151
Psychologists say there are only 5 kinds of people in the world. Which one are you?	152 e 153

Focus on culture	154 a 157
How do Brazilians spend their money?	154 e 155
How's the weather?	156 e 157
Language court	158 a 167
Irregular verbs	168 a 171
Glossary	172 a 176

UNIT 1
HOW MUCH IS IT?

Becky Bloom

Andrea Sachs

Henry Spencer

||| Get ready |||

1) What are the people in the pictures doing?

a) ◯ Buying books.   c) ◯ Buying food.

b) ◯ Buying clothes.   d) ◯ Buying furniture.

2) Which character seems worried about the item's price?

_____

3) What clothing items can you see in the pictures? Check all that apply.

a) ◯ Bag.   h) ◯ Hat.   o) ◯ Sunglasses.
b) ◯ Blazer.   i) ◯ High heels.   p) ◯ Sweater.
c) ◯ Blouse.   j) ◯ Jacket.   q) ◯ Tie.
d) ◯ Coat.   k) ◯ Jeans.   r) ◯ Wallet.
e) ◯ Dress.   l) ◯ Pants/Trousers. s) ◯ Wristwatch.
f) ◯ Glasses.   m) ◯ Shirt.   t) ◯ Purse.
g) ◯ Gloves.   n) ◯ Shoes.

Galahad and Gary Unwin

CHAPTER 1

Let's practice

1 Can you identify these items? Write the right names under the pictures.

> belt • boots • cap • dress • flip-flops • gloves • hat • high heels
> jacket • jeans • pajamas • pants • scarf • shirt • shorts • skirt
> socks • sneakers • sunglasses • T-shirt

a)
_____

b)
_____

c)
_____

d)
_____

e)
_____

f)
_____

g)
_____

h)
_____

i)
_____

j)
_____

k)
_____

l)
_____

m)
_____

n)
_____

o)
_____

p)
_____

q)
_____

r)
_____

s)
_____

t)
_____

Ilustrações: Marcelo Azalim

Let's listen n' speak

1. What is Kristen wearing today? Listen and circle the correct picture.

2. Listen to the interview again and complete the dialogue with the missing words.

> boots • clothes • comfortable • hat
> jacket • jumper • scarves • shirt
> shorts • sneakers • socks • winter

Interviewer: Welcome to *Chat with a Star*. Today our guest is Kristen Duran. Hi, Kristen, thank you for coming today.

Kristen: Hi, Lauren! I'm very happy to join you today.

Interviewer: So, I am aware you are a huge fan of wearing comfortable _____, right?

Kristen: Yes, I am.

Interviewer: Can you talk a little bit about what you are wearing today to our listeners?

Kristen: Sure. Today I'm wearing very light, _____ clothes. I'm wearing a pair of black cotton _____ and a blue and white _____. I'm also wearing a pair of white _____.

Interviewer: You look very comfortable, indeed! So, can you tell us what your favorite season is?

Kristen: Hum… Well, I enjoy summer days like today, but I really love _____.

Interviewer: Why do you prefer winter?

Kristen: I love winter because I can wear my leather _____ and colorful _____. When it's really cold, I wear a wool _____ and thick wool _____, and when it snows – what I love, by the way – I like to put on my red _____ and my black _____!

Interviewer: You are a very fashionable woman, so…

9

3 Board game. Have fun playing this game in small groups.

Clothing Board Game

START
What am I wearing?
What are you wearing?
What do you wear on a school day?
Move ahead a space
What were the last clothes you bought?
Move ahead a space
Do you always try on clothes before you buy them?
What´s your favorite piece of clothing? Describe it
Back to start
Do you prefer sandals or high heels?
What do you wear to go to sleep?
What am I wearing? A hat or a cap?
Name three traditional clothing from around the world
Which do you prefer: flip-flops or sneakers?
Skip a turn
What clothes would you never wear? Why?
What kind of clothes do you buy most frequently?
Do you prefer to shop or just to browse around? Why?
What is the strangest fashion trend you have ever seen?
FINISH

▶ **EXPLORING**

- *Bee Movie*, 2007.
- *Robots*, 2005.
- *The Lorax*, 2012.
- *The Princess and the Frog*, 2009.
- *Toy Story 3*, 2010.

CHAPTER 2 — Let's practice

1 Complete the sentences using **this**, **that**, **these** or **those**.

a) Where is _____ brown jacket?

b) Do you like _____ shorts?

c) I think _____ is an ugly shirt.

d) Where are _____ red sandals of yours?

LANGUAGE PIECE

Demonstrative pronouns
That — singular, far.
This — singular, near.
Those — plural, far.
These — plural, near.

2 Circle the correct option.

a)

Client: How much (is / are) (this / these) rings?
Clerk: (This are / These are) $ 14 each.

c)

Client: Thanks. Oh, just one more thing. How much (is / are) (this / these) silver bracelet?
Clerk: Sorry, but (this / that) is not for sale.
Client: Oh, sorry. I'll take only the sunglasses.

b)

Client: How about (that / those) sunglasses?
Clerk: (That / Those) are $ 35.

d)

Clerk: Here you are.
Client: Thank you!

3 Fill in the blanks with **how much is** or **how much are**.

a) _____ that bracelet?

b) _____ those ties?

c) _____ these socks?

d) _____ this wristwatch?

e) _____ these shoes?

f) _____ that skirt?

g) _____ the T-shirts?

h) _____ the red sweatshirt?

LANGUAGE PIECE

How much – interrogative form
How much is used to make questions about prices.
How much is – singular items.
How much are – plural items.

4 Write questions and answers with **how much**.

a) orange pullover / $ 74

_____

_____

b) green boots / $ 50

_____

_____

c) black leather pants / $ 92

_____

_____

d) white blouse / $ 37

_____

_____

5 Connect the questions to their possible answers.

a) How much are these?

b) How much is this?

◯ It is ten dollars.

◯ They are eighteen dollars.

◯ It is six dollars.

◯ The socks are six dollars.

◯ The blouse is fifty dollars.

◯ They are six.

◯ This jacket is fifteen dollars.

◯ These are eighteen dollars.

◯ The dress is forty dollars.

◯ Those shoes are twenty dollars.

Let's listen n' speak

1 Listen to the dialogue and check the best option.

a) Whose birthday is it today?
- ◯ Amanda's.
- ◯ Michelle's.
- ◯ Dad's.

b) How much does Amanda have?
- ◯ $ 78.00.
- ◯ $ 86.00.
- ◯ $ 68.00.

c) How much are the black boots?
- ◯ $ 127.00.
- ◯ $ 117.00.
- ◯ $ 80.00.

d) How much are the brown boots?
- ◯ $ 18.00.
- ◯ $ 80.00.
- ◯ $ 8.00.

2 Complete with the missing information.

a) Amanda is _____.

b) The gloves are _____.

c) The jacket is _____.

d) On the two pairs of gloves, Amanda is spending _____.

3 Now Amanda is visiting a bookstore. Complete the dialogue using **how much is**, **how much are**, **it's** or **they're**:

Amanda: Wow! There are lots of great books! _____ this small cooking book?

Salesperson: _____ $ 5.

Amanda: Great! And let me see… I love romances! _____ the romances?

Salesperson: _____ $ 20 each. Oh, look, this one is on sale. _____ only $ 10.

Dad: Look, Amanda! A biography of your favorite pop star!

Amanda: Ohh, cool! _____ it, please?

Salesperson: _____ $ 40.

Amanda: Oh… I don't have enough money.

Dad: I can help you, dear! Here you are, two dollars.

Amanda: Great!

4 Working in pairs, role-play a dialogue in a store. Remember to exchange roles. Be creative!

Let's practice

1 Complete the chart writing the clothes under the correct category.

> coat • cold • get dressed • gloves • hat • put on • raincoat
> rainy • skirt • stormy • suit • sunglasses • sunny • sweater
> take • take off • try on • umbrella • wear • windy

Weather	Things we do / Actions	Clothes / Objects

2 Match the names of the shops and their definitions.

- ( ) a shop that sells bread and cakes.
- ( ) a store that sells at cheap prices or for less than the original price.
- ( ) a very small shop where you can buy newspapers, chocolates, services etc.
- ( ) a small structure on a street that sells newspapers and magazines.

a) Kiosk
b) Retail outlet
c) Newsstand
d) Bakery

TRACK 03

Vocabulary hint
Numbers
Pay close attention to the correct pronunciation of the following numbers and never slip up when talking about prices or shopping.

3	15	60
13	50	9
30	6	19
5	16	90

3 Orally, list in Portuguese other places where you can shop. Then, pair up with a friend to write down on a separate sheet a definition for each of them. Use a dictionary to translate into English the list of places and their definitions. Hand it in to the teacher.

14

Let's read n' write

1 Read the following tale and answer the questions.

■ TALES & STORIES

The Emperor's New Suit
by Hans Christian Andersen (1837)

Many, many years ago lived an emperor, who thought so much of new clothes that he **spent** all his money in order to **obtain** them; his only ambition was to be always **well dressed**. He did not care for his soldiers, and the **theatre** did not **amuse** him; the only thing, in fact, he thought anything of was **to drive out** and show a new suit of clothes. He had a coat for every hour of the day; and as one would say of a king "He is in his **cabinet**", so one could say of him "The emperor is in his **dressing-room**".

The great city where he resided was very **gay**; every day many strangers from all parts of the globe arrived. One day two **swindlers** came to this city; they made people believe that they were **weavers**, and declared they could manufacture the finest **cloth** to be imagined. Their colours and patterns, they said, were not only exceptionally beautiful, but the clothes made of their material possessed the wonderful quality of being invisible to any man who was **unfit** for his office or unpardonably stupid.

"That must be wonderful cloth", thought the emperor. "If I were to be dressed in a suit made of this cloth, I should be able to find out which men in my empire were unfit for their places, and I could distinguish the clever from the stupid. I must have this cloth **woven** for me without delay." […]

Hans Christian Andersen. *The Emperor's New Suit*.
Available at: <http://hca.gilead.org.il/emperor.html#>. Access: July 2018.

GLOSSARY

Amuse (to amuse): divertia (divertir).
Cabinet: gabinete.
Cloth: tecido.
Dressing-room: camarim.
Gay: alegre.
Obtain (to obtain): obter (obter).
Spent (to spend): gastava (gastar).
Swindlers: vigaristas, trapaceiros(as).
Theatre: teatro.
To drive out: sair.
Unfit: impróprio(a).
Weavers: tecelões.
Well dressed: bem vestido(a).
Woven (to weave): tecida (tecer).

a) What is the text about?

- ○ It is about a king.
- ○ It is about an empress.
- ○ It is about a queen.
- ○ It is about an emperor.

b) What did the emperor love the most? Mark it.

c) How much did the emperor spend on his hobby? How do you know that?

_____

_____

d) Who arrives in the city? Are they trustworthy?

- ◯ Two swindlers. They are trustworthy.
- ◯ Two seamstress. They aren't trustworthy.
- ◯ Two seamstress. They are trustworthy.
- ◯ Two swindlers. They aren't trustworthy.

e) What is special about the clothes the newcomers say they design?

_____

_____

f) What are the attributes the emperor thought the clothes had?

_____

_____

_____

2 What is the genre of this text?

- **a)** ◯ Romance.
- **b)** ◯ Report.
- **c)** ◯ Tale.
- **d)** ◯ Biography.
- **e)** ◯ Poetry.
- **f)** ◯ Thriller.

3 What type of text is it?

- **a)** ◯ Descriptive.
- **b)** ◯ Narrative.
- **c)** ◯ Expository.

4 Check all the characteristics that apply to this kind of text genre.

a) ◯ argumentation d) ◯ characters g) ◯ sequence
b) ◯ description e) ◯ plot h) ◯ setting
c) ◯ information f) ◯ rhyme

5 Now it is your turn. Get ready to rewrite the emperor's tale creating a new story for it. Check the following tips, follow your teacher's instructions and use your imagination.

Pay attention to some tips:

1. Take notes on the key elements of the story;
2. Decide what you are going to change;
3. Define a new setting and context;
4. Set up the new plot;
5. Create a new conflict and tension;
6. Create a new crisis or climax.

Writing a draft

Outline the plot before you begin. Write up a quick list of the major plot elements you are going to change in the story and check if they make sense. Start your story rewriting a draft, so you can check if everything works well with your new story.

Revising your essay

Revise your writing. Revision is the most important part of writing.

Take notes!

_____
_____
_____
_____

Chapter 4

||| Citizenship moment |||

Culture

In pictures: traditional dress around the world

The Sari, India

Ostensibly the simplest item of clothing possible – a single **length** of fabric, up to nine metres long – the sari is also one of the world's most versatile and stylish **garments**, which can be **drapped** in dozens of different ways. The sari **spans** all of Indian society [...].

Kilts, Scotland

[...] The kilt has been used to represent all things Scottish [...]; visit any Scottish Highland Games, and you'll see that kilt-wearing traditions are alive and well, from the immaculately dressed competitive dancers to the **pipe** players in formal attire and, most impressively of all, the participants in the "heavy events" [...]

Balinese temple dress, Indonesia

Anyone visiting a Balinese temple should at least wear two basic elements of Balinese traditional dress, a sash (*selendang*) and a sarong-style skirt known as a *kain* [...].

Maasai beadwork, Kenya

One of the smaller ethnic groups in Kenya, but one of the most recognisable, the Maasai's reputation worldwide **belies** its size, no small part thanks to their stunning **attire**: brilliant red **cloth**, extraordinarily intricate **beadwork** and – for young men – long, ochre-dyed hair. [...]

Gho, Bhutan

In Bhutan, [...] it's obligatory for everyone to wear the national dress. For men this means the gho, a knee-length **gown** tied at the waist by a belt called a keram. For formal occasions a **silk** scarf, a kabney, is added to the ensemble, the colour of which depends on the **wearer**'s status. For the women, traditional dress is typically an ankle-length dress called a *kira*, and the equivalent scarf is called a *rachus*. [...]

GLOSSARY

Attire: traje.
Beadwork: bordado de contas.
Belies (to belie): desmente (desmentir).
Cloth: tecido.
Drapped (to drap): drapejado (drapejar).
Garments: vestuário.
Gown: vestimenta, vestido.
Length: comprimento.
Ostensibly: ostensivamente.
Pipe: gaita (de foles).
Silk: seda.
Spans (to span): abrange (abranger).
Wearer: portador(a).

The keffiyeh, shemagh or ghutrah, the Middle East

The scarf **headdress** worn by men across the Middle East comes in many variation of colour, style and name. It's known as shemagh in Jordan and the ghutrah in Saudi Arabia, where it is normally either white or red and white, and held in place by the agal, a black band. However, the Palestinian black-and-white keffiyeh is the most recognizable verson, having been appropriated worldwide both as a symbol of protest and a fashion item [...].

Kimono, Japan

Meaning 'the thing worn', kimonos are the ultimate symbol of traditional Japanese culture. From the seventeenth century **onwards** they developed as the main item of dress for men and woman, and a means of expression for the individual wearer. They are still worn for special occasions, such as weddings [...].

Alice Park. *In pictures: traditional dress around the world.*
Available at: <www.roughguides.com/gallery/traditional-dress/>. Access: July 2018.

> **GLOSSARY**
> **Headdress:** touca.
> **Onwards:** em diante.

Let's practice

1 Where is this clothing from? Match the columns.

a) Kabney • Indonesia
b) Kain   • Bhutan
c) Kimono • Japan
d) Sari   • India

2 Mark **T** (true) or **F** (false) according to the text.

a) ( ) The beadwork of the Maasai people is very little known around the world.

b) ( ) The tradition of wearing kilts is still true during the Scottish Highland Games.

c) ( ) The Balinese traditional dress is formed only by the *sash* and a sarong-style skirt.

d) ( ) The scarf headdress worn by men across the Middle East is known as keffiyeh, shemagh or ghutrah.

> **PROJECT**
>
> **Brazilian Traditional Attire**
> Team up in five groups. Each group will research the traditional clothing items of a Brazilian region. Go deep in the research and find out all the history behind each traditional clothing item. Gather all the information and some illustrative pictures of it. Then, gather all the groups' information and make a Brazilian Traditional Attire reference book.

> **EXPLORING**
>
> • *Clothes around the World*, by Clare Lewis. Heinemann Library.
> • *What we wear: dressing up around the world*, by Maya Ajmera, Elise Hofer Derstine, Cynthia Pon. Charlesbridge.

||| Get ready |||

1 What do these images have in common?

_____

_____

2 Do you think these food items are healthy? Underline the healthy items with blue color and the junk food with red color.

> apple • bacon • banana • bread • cake • carrot
> cheese • chicken • cookie • egg • fish • grape
> hamburger • jam • juice • meat • milk • noodle
> oat • onion • papaya • pear • pie • pineapple
> sandwich • sausage • strawberry • syrup • tea
> watermelon • zucchini

Tiana

CHAPTER 1

Let's practice

1) Fill in the blanks and complete the food names.

a) c__ic__e__

b) __a__s

c) __a__a__a

d) __om__t__

e) __ttu__

f) __h__s__

g) e__s

h) r__c__

i) __a

j) __a__b__g__

k) w__r

l) b__t__r

m) p__t__t__

n) b__d

o) c__r__t

p) on__

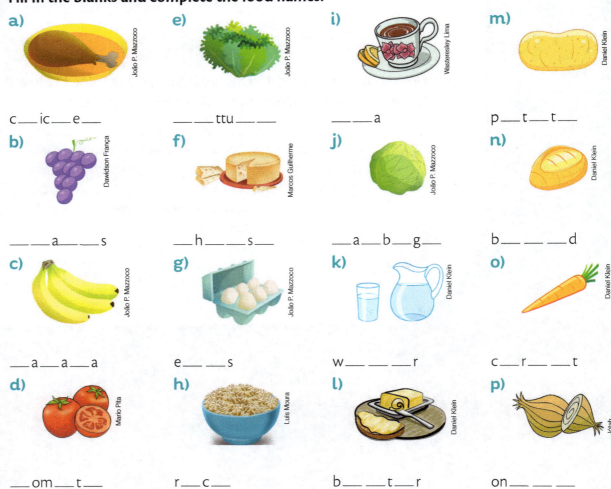

2) Organize the following words into the correct category.

bread • broccoli • butter • cake • carrot • cheese • chocolate • coffee • cookie • egg • garlic • ham • milk • pasta • pineapple • rice • steak • tea • tomato • water • watermelon

Drinks	Meat and eggs	Sweets, fats and oils	Vegetables	Fruits	Dairy products	Grains

22

3 When do you usually eat this? Look at the pictures and write **B** for breakfast, **L** for lunch and **D** for dinner.

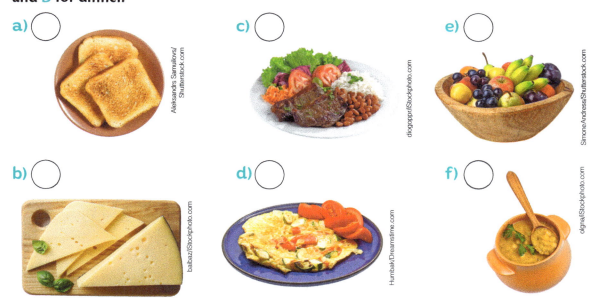

4 Complete the crossword with the name of the food items.

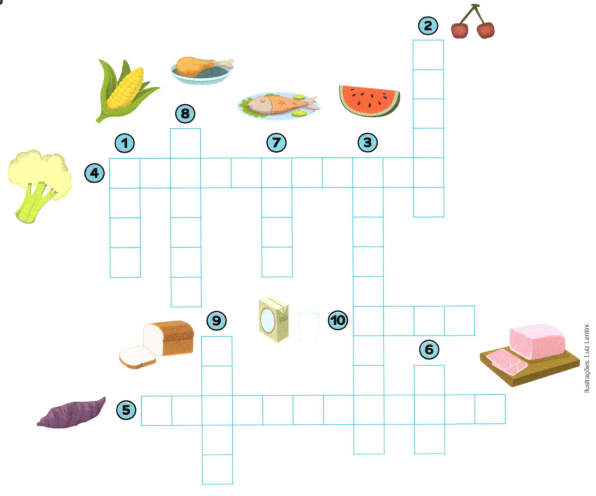

Let's listen n' speak

TRACK 04

1 Grocery list. Listen to the dialogue and circle all the items Chris has to buy.

2 Listen to the audio again and answer the questions.

a) Where is Chris going to go?

- ◯ To the supermarket.
- ◯ To the grocery store.
- ◯ To the shopping mall.

b) Based on the ingredients Chris is going to buy, circle what she and Nat are having for dinner.

3 Let's talk. Practice speaking with a friend by interviewing each other. Answer the following questions.

- What is your favorite meal?
- Do you often eat bread?
- Do you ever eat mustard, ketchup or mayonnaise?
- How often do you go to the supermarket?
- Do you ever write a shopping list? Why?
- What kind of food do you keep in the freezer?
- Have you ever smelled spoiled food? How does it smell?
- How often do you clean out your fridge?

CHAPTER 2

Let's practice

1 Observe the images and answer.

a) List all the food items you see.

_____

_____

b) Are all the ingredients counted by units?

_____

_____

c) Write in the chart which food items are counted by units and which ones are counted using measurement scale.

units counting		scale counting	

2 Complete using **a**, **an** or **some**.

a) There are _____ eggs in the fridge.

b) There isn't _____ orange to make _____ juice.

LANGUAGE PIECE

Countable and uncountable nouns

Countable nouns: Items that can be counted in units.

Uncountable nouns: Items that cannot be counted in units. They need words to express the quantity.

3 Choose the right options and fill in the blanks.

a) There weren't _____ vegetables left when I went to the farmer's market. (much / many)

b) There is _____ soda in the fridge. (some / any)

c) There is _____ soda in the bottle. (little / few)

d) He never eats _____ food for breakfast. (much / many)

e) Carla bought _____ strawberries. (little / few)

f) There are _____ mushrooms in my soup. (a little / a few)

g) Are there _____ chips to eat? (some / any)

h) I need _____ bit of sugar, please. (a little / a few)

> **LANGUAGE PIECE**
> **Quantifiers**
> | countable | uncountable |
> |---|---|
> | a/an | much |
> | numbers | little/a little |
> | many | some |
> | few/a few | any |
> | some | |
> | any | |

4 Correct the mistake in each sentence.

a) There isn't some bacon.

_____

b) Does she have much sandwiches?

_____

c) Would you like a soup?

_____

5 Let's play a memory game: **shopping bag**. Follow the instructions below and have fun!

- Form groups of 8 to 10 students.
- One student starts the game by saying: "At the supermarket I need to buy some fish.".
- The student next to him / her repeats the first sentence and adds something else to the list: "At the supermarket I need to buy some fish and some bananas.".
- Each student, in turns, repeats the sentence and adds an item. The students have to remember all the things in the correct order.

Let's listen n' speak

1 Listen to the dialogue and match the columns. Alicia can't go out with Jason...

a) tonight

b) on Saturday afternoon

c) on Sunday

d) next week

• ( ) because she has to wash her hair.

• ( ) because she needs to study math.

• ( ) because she needs to travel.

• ( ) because she has to take care of her brother.

2 Why didn't Alicia want to go to the movies? _____

3 What are Jason and Alicia doing tonight? _____

4 Role play the dialogue below, changing the underlined piece of information. Be creative!

Jason: Hey, Alicia! How are you doing?

Alicia: Hi, Jason! I'm fine, thanks. Nice to talk to you!

Jason: Listen, I want to ask you something... Would you like to go to the movies with me this afternoon?

Alicia: Sure! It will be great!

Jason: Cool. I want to see that new horror movie!

Alicia: Oh, well... Ahhn... Actually, I can't go. I'm sorry, Jason. I need to study for tomorrow's math test.

Jason: It's OK. What about Saturday afternoon? Do you want to watch that movie with me on Saturday afternoon?

Alicia: On Saturday?

Jason: Yes, on Saturday afternoon. I'd love to watch this movie with you!

Alicia: I'm sorry, but it won't be possible either. I have to wash my hair on Saturday.

Jason: Wash your hair? Oh, well... I see... Maybe on Sunday, then? Why don't we go to the movies on Sunday?

Alicia: Oh, I'd love to, but I'm busy on Sunday. I'm sorry. I have to take care of my brother...

Jason: Would you like to go to the movies next week?

Alicia: Oh, I'd really love to, but I can't. I need to travel next week.

Jason: Alicia, tell me... You don't want to go out with me, right?

Alicia: Oh, no, Jason! I really want to go out with you! It's just that... Well... Oh... Err... I'm really afraid of horror movies.

Jason: Ah, why didn't you say it before? Would you like to have dinner with me tonight?

Alicia: Sure!!!

Let's practice

1) Read the following invitations. Then, unscramble the words to write correct excuses.

a) Would you like to play baseball tonight? (work / I'm / have / sorry, / I / I / to / can't. / tonight.)
_____

b) Would you like to go dancing tomorrow? (broke. / I'm / sorry, / I / I'm / can't.)
_____

c) Would you like to go surfing? (I'm / sorry, / I / sick. / can't. / I'm)
_____

2) Use the information in parentheses and write excuses and invitations.

a) **Q:** (to go to the concert; tomorrow).
_____
_____
A: (to have to; to study).
_____
_____

> **Vocabulary hint**
> **Modal verb can**
> We **can** go to the party.
> **Can** you go to my house?
> They **can't** come with us.
> Of course she **can**.
> TRACK 06

b) **Q:** (to study at my house; this afternoon).
_____
_____

A: (to be feeling sick).
_____
_____

3) Read the following sentences and write **E** for excuses or **I** for invitations.

a) ( ) I'm sorry, I can't. I'm broke.   d) ( ) I'd love to, but I need to study.

b) ( ) Would you like to dance with me?   e) ( ) Do you want to go to the theater?

c) ( ) Do you want to go out with me tomorrow?   f) ( ) I'm sorry, I have plans for tonight.

Let's read n' write

1 What is this blog about? Read the text and answer the questions.

GLOSSARY

Avocado: abacate.
Chop (to chop): picar.
Cilantro: coentro.
Covered: coberto(a).
Cup: xícara, copo.
Diced (to dice): cortar em cubos.
Dry (to dry): seco(a), secar.

Fret (to fret): aborrecer-se.
Medium heat: fogo médio.
Hungry: faminto(a).
Mix (to mix): mexer.
Olive oil: azeite.
Pepper: pimenta.
Recipe: receita.

Remaining: que sobraram.
Season (to season): temperar.
Simmer (to simmer): cozinhar lentamente.
Tbsp (tablespoon): colher de sopa.
Toasted: torrado(a).
Trouble: problema.

29

a) What is the text about?

- ( ) Shopping list.
- ( ) Recipe.
- ( ) Movie review.
- ( ) Article.

b) What problem does the text present?

_____

c) What is the solution found?

_____

d) Does the mother think the recipe is easy or difficult to be prepared?

_____

e) Check the items of the recipe. Do you know all of them?

- ( ) Avocado.
- ( ) Butter.
- ( ) Tomato.
- ( ) Cilantro.
- ( ) Flour.
- ( ) Lemon.
- ( ) Garlic.
- ( ) Juice.
- ( ) Olive oil.
- ( ) Onion.
- ( ) Papaya.
- ( ) Quinoa.
- ( ) Vinegar.
- ( ) Water.
- ( ) Pepper.

_____
_____

f) Would you like to try the quinoa and avocado salad? What kind of salad do you like?

_____
_____

g) Is salad healthy food or junk food? Why?

_____
_____

h) Do you cook or help cooking at home? What kind of food do you usually make?

_____
_____
_____

2 Can you identify the steps that make the text a recipe?

_____

_____

3 Let's share experiences! Think about an easy recipe you know or you usually follow. Sit down and write the ingredients and how to make it. It can be in Portuguese.

PROJECT

How about writing a Class Recipe Book?

Choose a recipe of a dish you like. Write it down in English.

Exchange your recipe with a classmate, so you can correct each other's recipes.

Correct it as needed and hand it in to the teacher for the final checking.

As soon as all the recipes are correct, you can start decorating your recipe's page to be part of the book. Use pictures, illustrations etc.

4 Later, pair up with a friend and use a dictionary to translate the recipes into English. If you prefer, you can draw the steps of the recipe, just like in the text, and use few sentences to explain it. After finishing your tasks, share your recipes with other pairs and hand them in to your teacher.

||| Tying in |||

Available at: <https://garfield.com/comic/1985-12-22>. Access: July 2018.

Let's practice

GLOSSARY

Spit out (to spit out): cuspo (cuspir).

1) Have you ever read any of Garfield's comic strips?
_____

2) Take a quick look at the comic strip above. What is he doing?
_____
_____

3) There aren't many sentences in this story. How can you understand it?
_____
_____

Do you think Garfield is an interesting cat? Why (not)?

_____
_____

 On his plate, there are 3 different types of food. What are they?

_____
_____

 Where is the irony of the comic strip?

_____
_____

7 Match the food that Garfield eats and their different food groups.

a)

b)

c)

- protein

- grains

- fruit and vegetables

EXPLORING

Fruits and vegetables game
- www.digitaldialects.com/English/Fruit_audio.htm

EXPLORING

- *The cafeteria ABC: A Retro-Food & Alphabet Book*, by The Enthusiast and Danielle Marshal. The Enthusiast.

EXPLORING

- *Cloudy with a chance of meatballs 2*, 2013.

PROJECT

Nutritional facts

Choose two industrialized foods you eat regularly. Look for the nutritional information on their packages and take notes. For each category write down which of the two options seems to be the best. Use the charts below.

REVIEW

1 There are 12 hidden words at the word search below. Find them and place each word in its corresponding box.

F	N	K	S	J	X	E	T	E	E	N	W	O	U	G	O	W	N	E	C	G	N	J
P	S	A	U	S	A	G	E	T	X	K	R	M	L	Y	L	F	X	K	X	Y	K	N
E	O	C	N	U	H	J	L	K	C	C	I	P	B	W	C	U	P	J	I	W	C	U
T	R	L	G	S	H	O	Z	D	M	Q	S	Z	R	P	O	E	H	R	N	P	R	J
Y	T	N	L	Q	Y	D	M	W	D	H	T	T	M	O	A	P	C	D	L	O	H	E
O	L	M	A	U	O	I	E	O	X	S	W	K	E	N	T	E	A	I	M	N	S	A
A	B	U	S	W	T	Y	P	Y	D	J	A	G	Y	D	B	C	D	Y	X	D	J	N
T	J	H	S	T	R	E	K	T	N	I	T	T	Z	M	X	N	O	O	D	L	E	S
J	P	D	E	N	N	Z	D	O	J	P	C	O	M	I	F	P	V	Z	Z	I	P	N
D	G	A	S	U	C	Y	R	X	B	P	H	N	V	H	O	A	E	Y	O	H	P	U
E	L	O	Q	E	K	L	Y	O	Q	V	P	E	I	B	Q	M	S	L	Q	B	V	K
D	O	R	U	G	E	Y	T	G	M	L	K	M	Q	P	S	Y	R	U	P	G	L	I
E	V	C	I	G	H	J	L	K	C	C	F	P	B	W	F	U	P	J	I	W	C	U
T	E	M	M	S	O	Z	U	C	C	H	I	N	I	N	W	E	A	I	M	N	S	U
D	S	A	O	U	C	Y	R	X	B	P	W	N	V	H	O	A	E	T	I	E	P	U
T	R	L	N	S	K	R	I	N	I	R	A	Z	R	P	E	E	H	R	N	P	R	S

Food	Clothing items
1.	1.
2.	2.
3.	3.
4.	4.
5.	5.
6.	6.

34

2 Using the information below, write questions using how much or how many. Then, answer the questions using it's or they're.

a) Cake – $ 35.00

_____

_____

b) Strawberries – $ 4.99

_____

_____

c) Onions – $ 0.50 each

_____

_____

d) Watermelon – $ 9.99

_____

_____

3 Complete with a, an, some or any.

a) There is _____ man here who wants to talk to you for _____ minutes.

b) How much is _____ apple at that store? There aren't _____ apples at home and I want to buy _____ .

c) There isn't _____ milk at home. Please, honey, can you go to the supermarket and buy _____ milk, _____ rice, _____ pineapple and _____ avocado?

d) There is _____ bread on the table, but there isn't _____ cheese in the fridge.

4 Using would you like and the complements given, write invitations and excuses.

a) (play baseball – tomorrow) _____

(wounded) _____

b) (rock concert – next month) _____

(have no money) _____

c) (study with me – this evening) _____

(have a date) _____

d) (go bowling – on Saturday) _____

(have to help my parents) _____

35

DO NOT FORGET!

HOW MUCH...?

It's / They're...
- $ 20 – twenty
- $ 21 – twenty-one
- $ 30 – thirty
- $ 40 – forty
- $ 50 – fifty
- $ 60 – sixty
- $ 70 – seventy
- $ 80 – eighty
- $ 90 – ninety

IS – singular, countable and uncountable

ARE – plural, countable

VOCABULARY

CLOTHING ITEMS
SHOES: high heels – sneakers – flip flops – boots.
ACCESSORIES: bag – glasses – gloves – bracelet – hat – scarf – wristwatch – sunglasses – tie.
CLOTHES: jeans – pants – blazer – coat – shorts – shirt – T-shirt – dress – skirt – blouse – jacket – trousers – sweater – underwear.

FOOD
FRUITS: papaya – apple – grapes – pineapple – pear – watermelon – banana – strawberry.
VEGGIES: carrot – zucchini – onion.
PROTEIN: eggs – meat – fish – chicken – bacon.
YUMMY: cake – jam – bread – oat – cookies – hamburger – syrup.

DEMONSTRATIVE

THIS – near, singular
THAT – distant, singular
THESE – near, plural
THOSE – distant, plural

Would you like...? — **INVITATIONS:** "Would you like to go to the movies with me?".

QUANTIFIERS

COUNTABLE: many – few – a few – some – a/an numbers

UNCOUNTABLE: much – a little – little – some – any

A – a carrot, a boy, a car, a sausage...

AN – an apple, an orange, an egg...

SOME – affirmative/ interrogative countable/uncountable. There is some milk at home.

ANY – negative/interrogative countable/uncountable. There isn't any milk.

OVERCOMING CHALLENGES

(FGV – 2009)

UN STUDY FINDS BRAZIL'S WORKING CONDITIONS UNSATISFACTORY

A UN study released Monday pointed out that Brazil's current working conditions remain poor, though the country ____1____ a significant improvement in the past decade. According to the study, Brazil witnessed economic growth at the beginning of the decade ____2____ led to an increasing number of available jobs and a growth of workers' average incomes. But the study also finds that wage differences between men and women, blacks and non-blacks are still high.

In 2006, the average income of non-black women in Brazil was 524.6 reais (327.8 U.S. dollars), while that of black women was 367.2 reais (229.5 dollars). The average income of black men in 2006 was 451.1 reais (281.9 dollars), while that of non-black men was 724.4 reais (452.75 dollars). In addition, Brazilians aged between 16 and 24 face ____3____ difficulties in finding a job than any other age group, the study finds.

The study also shows that there are still 2.4 million children and teenager (aged 5-15) laborers in Brazil, ____4____ the number fell by 50 percent from 1992 to 2006.

September 9, 2008. <news.xinhuanet.com/english/2008-09/09/content_9867753.htm>. Acess: Oct. 2018.

Assinale a alternativa que completa corretamente a lacuna 3.

a) any **b)** some **c)** more **d)** as **e)** least

(PUC-PR – 2000)

Mark the CORRECT ALTERNATIVE to fill in the gaps of the dialogue below.

Wife: Do we need ____I____ wheat?
Husband: Yes, we do. We haven't got ____II____ wheat.
***
Husband: We need ____III____ apples, don't we?
Wife: No, we don't. We have got ____IV____ apples. But we have ____V____ carrots and ____VI____ cheese. Let's get some…

a) I – some; II – much; III – any; IV – few; V – many; VI – little

b) I – much; II – any; III – many; IV – too much; V – few; VI – few

c) I – few; II – some; III – little; IV – many; V – little; VI – little

d) I – any; II – much; III – some; IV – many; V – few; VI – little

e) I – few; II – many; III – few; IV – no; V – much; VI – many

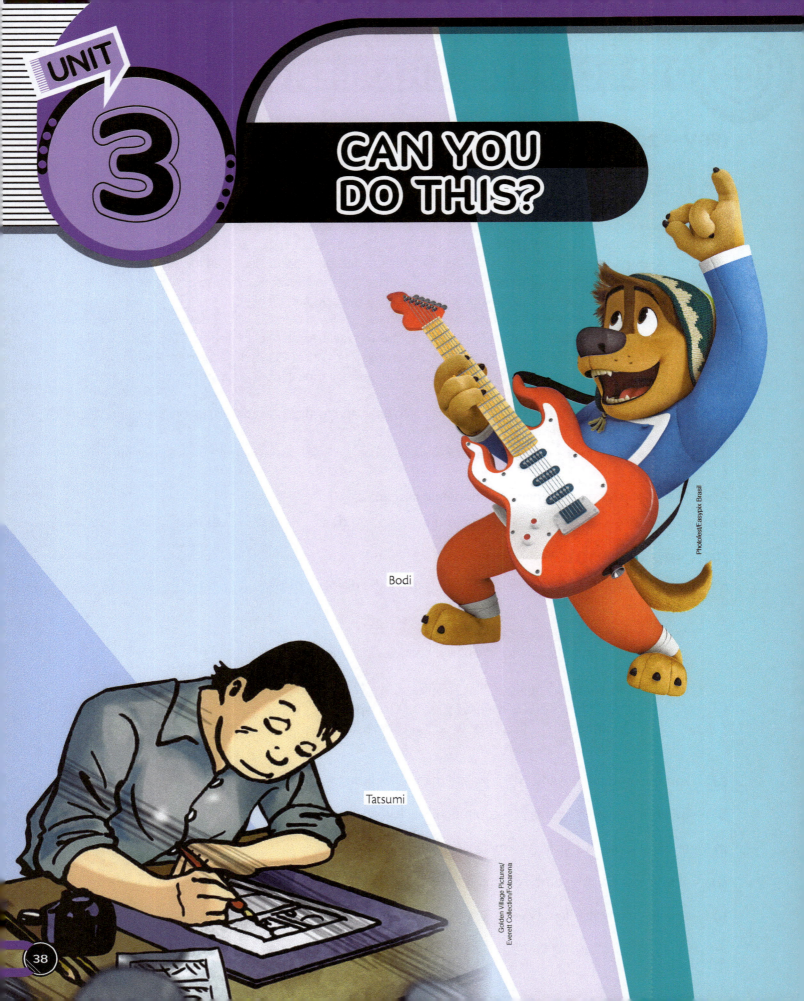

||| Get ready |||

1 What are these characters doing? Match.

a) Hiccup Horrendous Haddock III • singing

b) Bodi • playing the guitar

c) Félicie Milliner • drawing

d) Meena • dancing

2 Can you do any of these activities? If not, which one would you like to do?

_____

_____

3 Is there any activity you are good at? What ability would you like to have?

_____

_____

_____

Félicie

Meena

Chapter 1

Let's practice

1) What can they do? Name it.

> act • cook • dance • draw • drive • play an instrument
> ride a bicycle • run • sew • sing • swim • take pictures

a)

e)

i)

_____

_____

_____

b)

f)

j)

_____

_____

_____

c)

g)

k)

_____

_____

_____

d)

h)

l)

_____

_____

_____

2) Put the sentences in order and find out what these people can do.

a) can / Mirna / beautiful / draw / images

_____

b) play / the piano / Simon / the sax / can / and the drums

_____

c) for hours / can / swim / Susan

_____

d) pies / can / delicious / cook / Marcus

_____

e) a truck / My grandpa / drive / can

_____

f) a dress / can / Eleanor / in a day / sew

_____

3) Find the eleven abilities you saw on exercise 1 in the word soup.

Q	W	E	R	T	Y	U	I	O	P	A	R	D	F	G	H	J	K
P	L	A	Y	*	A	N	*	I	N	S	T	R	U	M	E	N	T
L	Z	X	C	V	B	N	M	L	K	J	A	H	G	F	D	S	A
R	C	V	B	N	M	Z	Q	W	E	R	K	T	Y	U	I	O	P
I	A	E	I	O	U	B	C	D	F	G	E	H	J	K	L	M	N
D	A	N	C	E	L	M	V	B	N	W	*	O	L	K	J	H	P
E	A	V	S	A	E	I	E	I	O	U	P	B	C	D	F	G	Q
M	B	U	C	S	W	I	M	O	P	Q	I	A	U	R	V	X	R
A	C	T	C	F	Y	O	U	T	S	R	C	E	C	A	X	Z	S
I	D	S	O	B	S	I	N	G	U	V	T	I	F	W	Z	W	T
B	E	R	O	N	E	A	A	B	C	D	U	O	H	T	W	Y	A
I	F	Q	K	V	B	N	S	H	G	F	R	D	R	I	V	E	C
C	G	P	O	E	I	O	E	K	L	M	E	D	U	J	O	Q	T
Y	H	O	O	J	K	L	W	M	L	K	S	Z	N	K	N	R	V

Let's listen n' speak

1) Look at these blog posts about people's skills. Listen to them and complete the blank spaces.

PEOPLE'S SKILLS

The artist
My name is Susan. I'm a painter and a graphic artist. I can _____ or _____ many different things.

The actor
I'm Robert. I'm an actor. I can _____ and I can _____. I can also _____ different musical instruments. I work on Broadway, New York.

The athlete
My name is Isadora and I'm an athlete. I can _____, I can _____, and I can _____ bicycle. I am on the Ironman competition.

The chef
My name is Zachary and I'm a chef. I can _____ many different food and dishes. I can _____ cakes and cookies too.

2) Listen to the audio again and match the people to their abilities.

a) The chef
b) The athlete
c) The artist
d) The actor

• paint and draw.
• cook and bake.
• sing, dance, and play.
• swim, run, and ride.

CHAPTER 2

Let's practice

1 Look at Sophie's story. According to it, what can she do now?

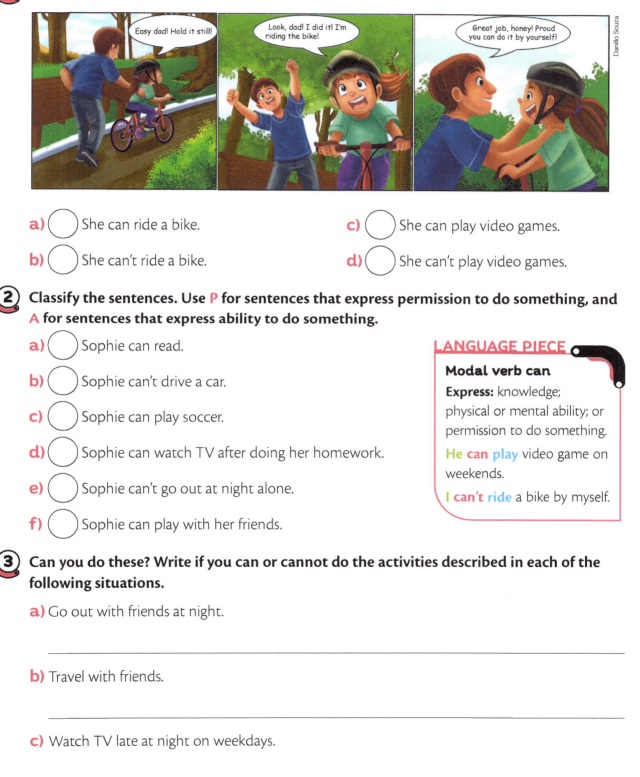

a) ◯ She can ride a bike.

b) ◯ She can't ride a bike.

c) ◯ She can play video games.

d) ◯ She can't play video games.

2 Classify the sentences. Use **P** for sentences that express permission to do something, and **A** for sentences that express ability to do something.

a) ◯ Sophie can read.

b) ◯ Sophie can't drive a car.

c) ◯ Sophie can play soccer.

d) ◯ Sophie can watch TV after doing her homework.

e) ◯ Sophie can't go out at night alone.

f) ◯ Sophie can play with her friends.

LANGUAGE PIECE

Modal verb can

Express: knowledge; physical or mental ability; or permission to do something.

He **can** play video game on weekends.

I **can't** ride a bike by myself.

3 Can you do these? Write if you can or cannot do the activities described in each of the following situations.

a) Go out with friends at night.

_____

b) Travel with friends.

_____

c) Watch TV late at night on weekdays.

_____

43

4 Look at the pictures and write sentences about what these people can or can't do.

dance • drive • paint • ski

a) Sarah and Tom _____.

b) Derek _____.

c) They _____.

d) He _____.

5 Write suggestions using the vocabulary from the box and modal verbs should or shouldn't.

eat sweets • recycle garbage • tidy your room • use the cell phone

a) _____

b) _____

c) _____

d) _____

6 Look at the sentences below. Read carefully and choose the best option.

a) You _____ brush your teeth between meals. (should / shouldn't)

b) He _____ waste many hours in front of the computer. (should / shouldn't)

c) Everybody _____ wash the hands before eating. (should / shouldn't)

d) People _____ drink too much coffee. (should / shouldn't)

7 Rearrange the following sentences and use **should** or **shouldn't** to complete their meaning.

a) people / watch / less TV

_____

b) boys and girls / go / to different schools

_____

c) people / be / able to choose healthier food

_____

d) we / stop / consuming sugar in excess.

_____

e) we / be afraid / of traveling abroad.

_____

> **Vocabulary hint**
> **Modal verb should**
> They <u>should</u> drink water.
> You <u>shouldn't</u> watch a lot of TV.
> What <u>should</u> I do?
> <u>Shouldn't</u> we try to finish it now?

8 Complete the sentences with **should** or **shouldn't**.

a) If someone doesn't understand your language very well, you _____ speak so fast.

b) If you need a pen, you _____ say 'May I borrow your pen, please?'.

c) If people want to live until they're very old, they _____ eat a lot of cakes and chocolate.

d) In a big city, you _____ be careful with your bag.

e) When you're traveling by car, you _____ drive for hours without stopping.

> **LANGUAGE PIECE**
> **Modal verb should**
> **Express:** the right thing to be done.
> He **should do** his homework first.
> I **shouldn't eat** candy before dinner.

Let's listen n' speak

1) Listen to the messages Patricia and Jane left for each other and answer.

a) What is Patricia trying to schedule with Jane?

_____

b) When does Patricia want to have the meeting with Jane?

- ◯ Tuesday, 3 p.m.
- ◯ Thursday, 3 p.m.
- ◯ Thursday, 3 a.m.

c) Does Jane agree or disagree with the time proposed by Patricia?

- ◯ She agrees.
- ◯ She disagrees.
- ◯ It doesn't say.

d) Does Jane agree with the meeting date Patricia proposes?

_____

e) When does Jane want to have a meeting?

- ◯ Monday.
- ◯ Thursday.
- ◯ Tuesday.
- ◯ Friday.
- ◯ Wednesday.
- ◯ Saturday.

LANGUAGE PIECE

Agree × disagree
Agree – share the same opinion.
Disagree – to have a different opinion.

2) Do they A (agree) or D (disagree) with each other?

a) ◯

Paula: We should get mom a nice birthday gift.
Jason: Sure! Let's go to the mall after lunch.

b) ◯

Sandra: I want to watch the new drama movie.
Daniel: Oh, I prefer the new action movie.

c) ◯

Katie: We should apply to the coding course.
John: Of course! We rock with logic.

d) ◯

Oscar: Hey, let's grab a pizza tonight!
William: I prefer something else like sushi.

3) Pair up and talk to a classmate about the following topics and find out if you agree or disagree about them.

- English is easy to learn.
- Everyone is good at something.
- There are no such things as ghosts.
- What goes around comes around.

Let's read n' write

1) Is flying a kite an ability or a skill? Can anyone learn how to fly a kite? Discuss with your classmates.

2) Now read the following Peanuts comic strip, and do as it is asked.

a) Say if the sentences are **T** (true) or **F** (false).

- ◯ Charlie Brown can fly his kite.
- ◯ Charlie Brown believes he cannot fly his kite.
- ◯ Lucy believes Charlie Brown can fly his kite.
- ◯ Lucy advises Charlie Brown to believe he can fly his kite.

b) According to Lucy, what is Charlie Brown's trouble?

_____

_____

GLOSSARY
Actually: realmente.
Ahead: em frente.
Bet: apostar.
Kite: pipa.
Out loud: em voz alta.
Over and over: repetidamente.

c) What is Lucy's piece of advice to Charlie Brown?

_____

d) How is Lucy's piece of advice going to help Charlie Brown?

_____

_____

e) Does Lucy believe Charlie Brown has the ability to fly his kite? Justify you answer.

_____

_____

f) Did Lucy behave in a good way with Charlie Brown? Justify your answer.

_____

_____

3 Read the comic strip again and analyse it. Then, answer the following questions.

a) What elements are there in the comic strip?

_____

_____

b) How are the characters' speeches presented?
- ◯ By speech bubbles.
- ◯ By thought bubbles.
- ◯ By narrator bubbles.

c) How is the story organized?
- ◯ By a narrative text.
- ◯ By a sequence of drawings.
- ◯ By a sequence of drawings and dialogues.

4 What about creating your own comic strip? Follow the instructions and have fun!

> Think about an ability or skill you have studied throughout this unit and use it as the theme for a comic strip.
>
> **In pairs:**
> - brainstorm how to use the ability in the comic strip;
> - brainstorm a fun element related to this theme;
> - brainstorm a sequence of events for the story;
> - think about the dialogues and onomatopoeias you can use in it;
> - detail the drawings of each scene and all the other elements it should have.

Now, on your own, get your version for the comic strip made up!

CHAPTER 4

||| Citizenship moment |||

THE TYPES OF INTELLIGENCE

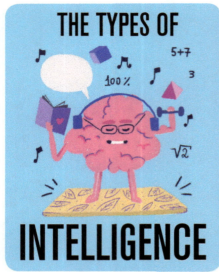

INTERPERSONAL

GOOD AT: sensing people's feelings and motives. **ENJOYS:** reading, organizing, and mediating. **NEEDS:** social interactions.

BODILY-KINESTHETIC

GOOD AT: coordinating mind with body. **ENJOYS:** physical activities. **NEEDS:** tactile experiences and hands-on learning.

LINGUISTIC

GOOD AT: finding the right words to express what mean. **ENJOYS:** reading, writing, telling stories, and word games. **NEEDS:** books, writing tools, debates, and dialogues.

INTRA-PERSONAL

GOOD AT: understanding yourself, what you feel, and what you want. **ENJOYS:** setting goals, meditating, and being quiet. **NEEDS:** time alone, self-paced projects, and choices.

VISUAL-SPATIAL

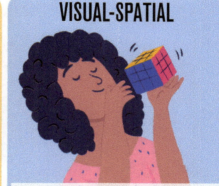

GOOD AT: visualizing the world in 3D. **ENJOYS:** designing, drawing, and visualizing. **NEEDS:** imagination games, puzzles, and art material.

MUSICAL

GOOD AT: discerning sounds, their pitch, tone, rhythm, and timbre. **ENJOYS:** singing, listening, and rhythm. **NEEDS:** contact with music and musical instruments.

LOGICAL-MATHEMATICAL

GOOD AT: quantifying things, making hypotheses and proving them. **ENJOYS:** experimenting, questioning, and calculating. **NEEDS:** things to explore, manipulative and science-related materials.

GLOSSARY

Hands-on learning: aprendizagem prática.
Kinesthetic: cinestésico.
Pitch: altura do som (grave ou agudo).
Puzzles: quebra-cabeças.
Setting (to set): estabelecendo (estabelecer).
Tactile: tátil.
Tools: ferramentas.

Ilustrações: Cristiane Viana

Based on: *Multiple Intelligences*, available at: <https://www.theodysseyonline.com/multiple-intelligences-in-the-classroom>; *Multiple Intelligence for adult literacy and education*, availabe at: <http://www.literacynet.org/mi/intro/index.html>. Access: July 2018.

Let's practice

1 **Read the following sentences about people's abilities and try to identify their main intelligence type.**

a) I'm very good at writing essays and understanding written texts.

_____

b) Kevin has always been a calm person with amazing knowledge of understanding himself.

_____

c) I'm musical self-taught. It has always been simple for me to understand music notes and rhythm.

_____

d) Pedro is a perfect leader. He is able to connect and understand people as nobody else.

_____

e) Carl is very good at logic thinking and writing codes.

_____

f) Susan is very good at reading maps and localizing herself geographically.

_____

g) Lilian and Martina are highly qualified synchronized swimmers.

_____

PROJECT

Class Types of Intelligence Pie Chart

First, individually, take the test your teacher will apply to you. Once you get the results, collectively, rank the results with your teacher's mediation. Once you get all the results from your class, analyze them and calculate the percentage of each intelligence type in your class. Finally, get all these percentages and make a pie chart of them.

EXPLORING

- *The Berenstain Bears – Show some respect*, by Jan Berenstain, Mike Berenstain. Zonderkidz.
- *What is respect?*, by Etan Boritzer. Veronica Lane Books.

EXPLORING

- *Dr. Seuss: The Lorax*, 2012.
- *Kindness is contagious*, 2015.

||| Get ready |||

1 What is the image about?

- ◯ Country map.
- ◯ Neighborhood map.
- ◯ City map.

2 Which of the following places can you identify in the map?

- **a)** ◯ Hospital.
- **b)** ◯ Gas station.
- **c)** ◯ Bank.
- **d)** ◯ City Hall.
- **e)** ◯ Library.
- **f)** ◯ School.
- **g)** ◯ Restaurant.
- **h)** ◯ Museum.
- **i)** ◯ Cinema.
- **j)** ◯ Supermarket.
- **k)** ◯ Parking lot.
- **l)** ◯ Fire department.
- **m)** ◯ Shops.
- **n)** ◯ Mall.
- **o)** ◯ Church.
- **p)** ◯ Beach.
- **q)** ◯ Park.
- **r)** ◯ Hotel.
- **s)** ◯ Post office.
- **t)** ◯ Bakery.
- **u)** ◯ Sports center.

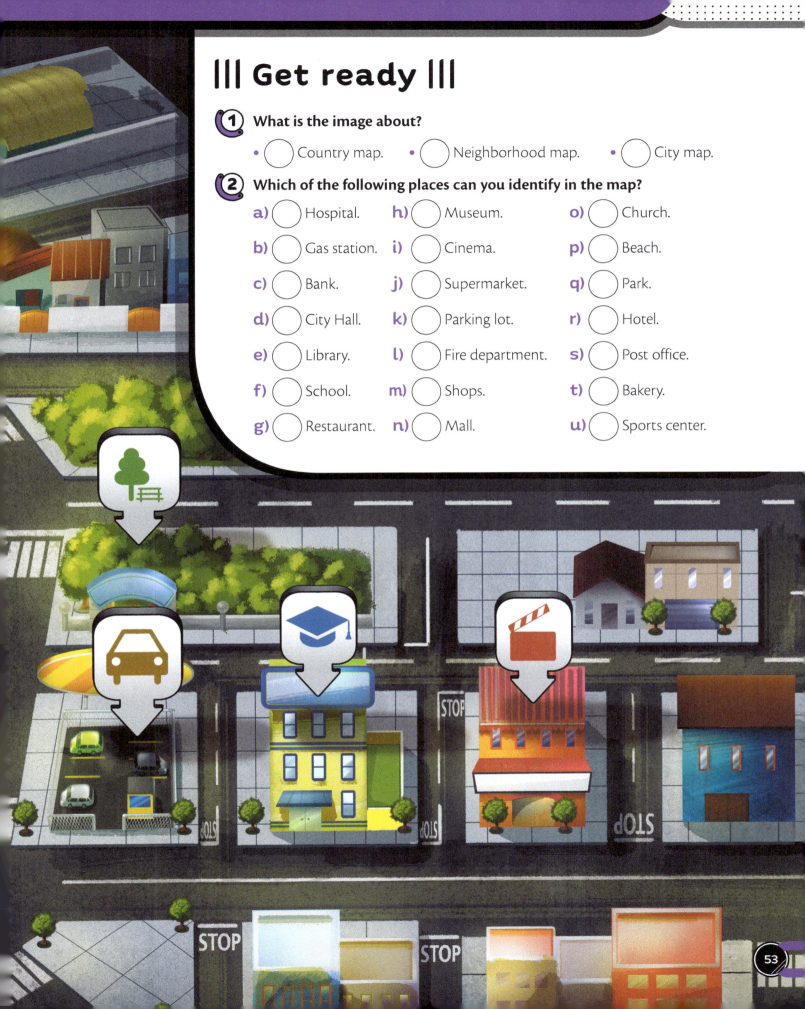

CHAPTER 1

Let's practice

1. Where do we do these things? Look at the city map, match the places with their definitions and name them.

a) ◯ A place where you can eat. _____

b) ◯ A place where children go to learn. _____

c) ◯ A place where people go to buy clothes, shoes. _____

d) ◯ An office where police officers work. _____

e) ◯ A place where you go to watch a movie. _____

f) ◯ A building where people go to pray. _____

g) ◯ A place where you go to send letters. _____

h) ◯ A place where doctors and nurses work. _____

i) ◯ A big shop where you can buy food and other things. _____

j) ◯ A building where people can see works of art. _____

k) ◯ A place where people can borrow books. _____

l) ◯ A place where people can buy groceries. _____

m) ◯ A place where people can buy medicines. _____

n) ◯ A place where people keep their money safe. _____

2 Look at the map and use there is or there are to describe each block.

a) _____
b) _____
c) _____
d) _____
e) _____
f) _____
g) _____
h) _____
i) _____
j) _____
k) _____
l) _____

LANGUAGE PIECE

There is × There are
Used to say that something exists or does not exist.
There is – singular. **There are** – plural.

3 Complete the sentence with the correct adjective.

bored • clean • excited • modern • noisy • old • polluted • quiet

a) Governments should solve the problem of _____ water because in a few years there is not going to be enough _____ water to everybody.

b) Sadie is so _____ about being at the beach on vacations because she was too _____ at work.

c) I am studying at the library because it is very _____ here. At home it is too _____, because my brother is rehearsing with his band.

d) Twenty years ago, there was an _____ house here, but there is a new _____ building now.

55

Let's listen n' speak

1) Listen to Sally talking about her city and tell if the sentences are **T** (true) or **F** (false).

a) ◯ Sally lives in a big, modern, and noisy city.

b) ◯ She loves the Italian restaurant she goes with her parents.

c) ◯ It's never difficult to move around the streets of Leicester.

d) ◯ Daniel lives in a small and old village.

e) ◯ There are lots of things to do in the city, like going to the theater, the cinema or the museums.

f) ◯ It is easy to get bored in the village. There is not much to do there.

2) Where can you find these things? Label them as **C** (city) or **V** (village).

a) ◯ Cars and buses.   e) ◯ Noise.   i) ◯ Rivers.

b) ◯ Cinemas.   f) ◯ Outdoor activities.   j) ◯ Theaters.

c) ◯ Museums.   g) ◯ Quiet.   k) ◯ Trees.

d) ◯ Nature.   h) ◯ Restaurants.   l) ◯ Waterfalls.

3) Answer the questions.

a) What can Sally do in the city?

_____

b) What is there near Daniel's house?

_____

c) What can people do in his village?

_____

4) It is your turn. Pair up and talk with a friend about the city or neighborhood you live in.

- Where do you live? – I live in _____.
- What places are there? – There are _____.
- What can you do there? – I can _____.
- What do you like and dislike the most about there? – I really like _____, but I dislike _____.

Let's practice

1 Look at the map and answer the questions using the preposition of place in brackets.

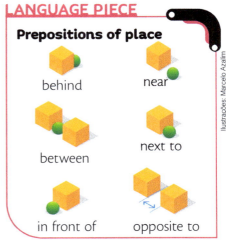

a) Where is the library? (next to)

_____

b) Where is the school? (behind)

_____

c) Where is the park? (opposite)

_____

d) Where is the drugstore? (in front of)

_____

2 Now, look at the previous map again and complete with the correct preposition.

a) The hospital is _____ the library.

b) The school is _____ the museum.

c) The restaurant is _____ the bank.

d) The store is _____ the supermarket and the drugstore.

e) The post office is _____ the school.

57

3 Based on the map below, choose the best options.

a) The doctors are (behind / in front of) the hospital.

b) The popcorn vendor is (on the corner of / behind) the school.

c) The ice cream shop is (in the same block of / two blocks away from) the bank.

d) The hospital is (next to / three blocks away from) the bank.

e) The church is (in front of / behind) the supermarket.

f) The park is (near / between) the library.

4 Say what direction it is.

a)

b)

c)

_____   _____   _____

5 On you notebook, write a few sentences using the prepositions of place and words to give directions.

6) How to get to the park...

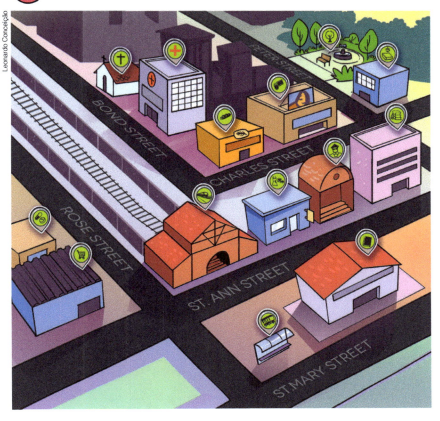

Vocabulary hint
Giving directions
behind　　　next to
between　　opposite to
go straight　turn left
in front of　turn right
near

a) ...from the church?

_____
_____

b) ...from the hospital?

_____
_____

c) ...from the store?

_____
_____

d) ...from the supermarket?

_____
_____

Let's listen n' speak

1 Listen to the conversation and label the following sentences as T (true) or F (false).

a) ◯ Amelia does not like Tokyo.

b) ◯ There is a lot of violence there.

c) ◯ Shibuya intersection is very busy.

d) ◯ Amelia lives in Kyoto.

e) ◯ People can play sports along the Sumida River Terrace.

2 Match the columns.

a) from Australia • ◯ Shibuya intersection

b) 1,000 pedestrians • ◯ Market of the Sun

c) it's just perfect • ◯ Amelia

d) modern • ◯ Sumida River Terrace

e) favorite monthly errand • ◯ skyscrapers

f) people can jog along • ◯ Tsukishima

3 Answer the questions.

a) Where does Amelia live in Tokyo? _____

b) What kind of buildings are there in Amelia's neighborhood?

_____

c) How many vendors are there at the Market of the Sun? _____

d) Where is the Market of the Sun? _____

4 Think of your neighborhood and talk to a partner about its places and what you can do in each of them.

> **Speaker A:** *There is a park near my house.*
> **Speaker B:** *What can people do there?*
> **Speaker A:** *People can run and work out at the outdoor gym.*

CHAPTER 3

Let's read n' write

1 Read the map and answer.

Based on: <www.nymap.net/content/maps-of-new-york-city/large-printable-tourist-attractions-map-of-Manhattan-New-York-city.jpg>. Access: July 2018.

a) Which city map is this?

_____

b) Check all the places you can see on the map.

- ◯ Bank
- ◯ Bridge
- ◯ Bus terminal
- ◯ Hospital
- ◯ Hotel
- ◯ Museum
- ◯ Park
- ◯ Post office
- ◯ River
- ◯ Supermarket
- ◯ School
- ◯ Restaurant

c) Which important landmarks can be visited on the 5th Avenue?

_____

_____

d) Which rivers surround the city?

- ◯ Byram River.
- ◯ East River.
- ◯ Harlem River.
- ◯ Mianus River.
- ◯ Silvermine River.
- ◯ Hudson River.

e) What's the way to visit the Statue of Liberty?

_____

(2) Talking about places in a city. Can you list the most common public places in your neighborhood?

_____

_____

(3) What would life be like without these commercial establishments? Why?.

_____

(4) Who are maps made for?

a) ◯ People who want information about a place.

b) ◯ People who want to forget how to go to places.

c) ◯ People who want to know how to go to places.

d) ◯ For people who know the area.

5 Do you use maps to move around your city? Why?

_____

6 Have you ever used any kind of online mapping service? What are the advantages and disadvantages of paper maps, web, and application services?

_____

7 When visiting a new place or city, would you want to use a map? Why?

_____

_____

8 Do you know how to make a map? Pair up with a friend, read the following text and elaborate a map showing all the important places of your school neighborhood.

How to – city maps

How to Design a City Map

Things You'll Need

- 20 by 28 centimeters white paper
- pencil
- colored pencils or crayons

Instructions

    Turn the paper on its side to create a rectangle. Using a regular pencil, **begin to draw** the basics, including streets and **well-known buildings** like the school, library or grocery store.

    Label all of the streets using a pencil, and label buildings or points of interest with the colored pencils. Designate a symbol for a particular building to create a **legend** later on.

    Color in the map as **desired** and create a **compass** and legend in one of the four corners. A compass with **N** (North), **S** (South), **E** (East) and **W** (West) will help know which direction points of interest are located **within** the city. For a legend, list all of the symbols and points of interest on the map as a **key** to remember what each of the colored symbols stand for.

GLOSSARY

Begin (to begin): comece (começar).
Buildings: prédios.
Compass: bússola.
Desired (to desire): desejado (desejar).
Key: chave.
Label (to label): nomeie (nomear).
Legend: legenda.
To draw: desenhar.
Turn (to turn): vire (virar).
Well-known: bem conhecido(a).
Within: dentro.

9 Now that you have your own map, write down some touristic information on how to go to places using your map.

||| Tying in |||

Your way under the ground

There are **several** ways **to get around** in a city. Walking, driving a car, riding on a bus, and even riding a bicycle. One very efficient means of transport you can find especially in big cities is the **subway** or **underground**, as it is called in England. Subways are **generally** fast, safe, practical, and comfortable. It does not **face traffic** and **allows** you to make many connections to get to your destination if needed. Here it is an example of a subway system. This is the map of Boston's subway, in the United States.

> **GLOSSARY**
>
> **Allows (to allow):** permite (permitir).
> **Face (to face):** enfrentar.
> **Generally:** geralmente.
> **Several:** vários(as).
> **Subway:** metrô.
> **To get around:** locomover-se.
> **Traffic:** trânsito.
> **Underground:** metrô (como é chamado na Inglaterra).

# Let's practice

1) **What do you know about subway systems? Observe the map and answer the questions:**

a) Where is this subway system map from? _____

b) What department designed this map? _____

c) How can you identify the different lines in the map? _____

d) How can you identify the stations? _____

2) **What is the way? Look at the map and say the directions to get to these destinations.**

a) You are at Alewife Station and want to go to Design Center Station.

_____

_____

b) You are at W. Roxbury Station and want to go to Wonderland Station.

_____

_____

_____

3) **In small groups, discuss the following topics.**

a) Is there a subway system in your city?

b) If so, does it work properly? What could be done to improve it?

c) If not, would it be a good choice of transportation? Why?

 **EXPLORING**

Metro and Underground Maps Designs around the World
- www.noupe.com/inspiration/metro-and-underground-maps-design-around-the-world.html

 **EXPLORING**

Brand New Subway
- http://jpwright.net/subway/

PROJECT

Brazilian Subway System

Team up and research about means of transportation in Brazil. Check for all the places that have subway systems, and then exchange information with your classmates.

65

REVIEW

1) What are their abilities? Look at the images and make affirmative, interrogative, and negative sentences using **can**.

a)

Affirmative: _____

Interrogative: _____

Negative: _____

b)

Affirmative: _____

Interrogative: _____

Negative: _____

c)

Affirmative: _____

Interrogative: _____

Negative: _____

2) Unscramble the words and write correct sentences.

a) good Albert drawing really at is.

_____

b) dancing I not am at good.

_____

c) can They the very guitar well play.

_____

d) at mother like be to good would singing My.

_____

_____

66

3 Look at the map and complete the sentences below with **there is**, **there isn't**, **there are** or **there aren't**.

a) _____ a café next to the restaurant.

b) _____ many trees in this city.

c) _____ any churches in this city.

d) _____ a cinema in this city.

4 Look at the map again and write if the sentences are **T** (true) or **F** (false).

a) ◯ The school is between the café and the restaurant.

b) ◯ The park is behind the buildings.

c) ◯ The school is next to the zoo.

d) ◯ The museum is in front of the amusement park.

5 Write questions for the following answers.

a) _____

I live on Baker street, next to the church.

b) _____

In my city, there are beautiful parks and museums.

c) _____

I don't like the traffic and the pollution.

d) _____

I would like to live in the countryside.

DO NOT FORGET!

I CAN/CAN'T...

- ACT
- COOK
- DANCE
- DRAW/PAINT
- DRIVE
- PLAY AN INSTRUMENT
- RIDE A BIKE
- RUN
- SEW
- SING

CAN

KNOWLEDGE OF HOW TO DO SOMETHING:
I can drive really well.

PHYSICAL OR MENTAL ABILITY TO DO SOMETHING:
She can speak three languages: English, Italian, and French!

POSSIBILITY OF DOING SOMETHING:
They can get a good grade if they study hard.

PERMISSION TO DO SOMETHING:
He can go to the concert tomorrow night.

SHOULD / SHOULDN'T

It is a good thing to do, the right thing.

Example: To be healthy, you should exercise often and you shouldn't eat junk food and sweets.

A CITY

Can be... clean or polluted · modern or old · quiet or noisy

IN THE CITY...

Where is / are the...?
- next to...
- behind...
- opposite...
- in front of...
- between...
- on the corner of...
- on the same block...
- near...

- bank(s)
- school(s)
- church(es)
- cinema(s)
- gas station(s)
- hospital(s)
- restaurant(s)
- supermarket(s)
- library(ies)

There is / isn't: singular.
There are / aren't: plural.

How can I get to the...?
- Go straight...
- Turn left on...
- Turn right on...

OVERCOMING CHALLENGES

(Eear – 2016)

Select the correct modal verb that fills in the blank in the paragraph below.

> Paul feels very sick and dizzy. I think he has been drinking all night again.
>
> He _____ get out of bed this morning.

a) will

b) must

c) can't

d) could

(UERJ – 2016)

And I **should** know. (panel 4)

Modal verbs can be used to refer to a speaker's attitude. The modal should indicates that Calvin believes his knowledge of the bad quality of the TV show would be characterized as:

a) desirable.

b) probable.

c) surprising.

d) mandatory.

UNIT 5
DID YOU READ THESE STORIES?

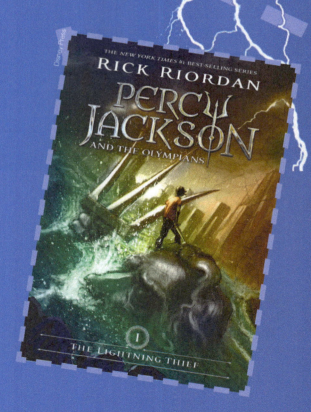
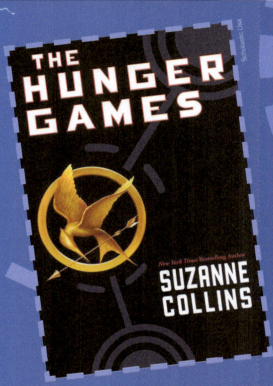
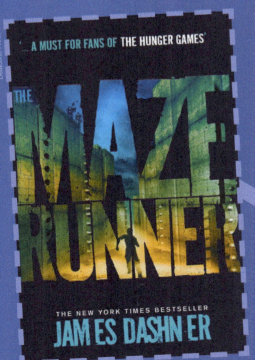

||| Get ready |||

1 Do you know any of these books? Exchange ideas with your classmates.

2 Can you say who the main characters in each story are? Discuss with your classmates:

3 Do you know the story of any of these books? Match.

a) The Lightning Thief.   **c)** The Golden Compass.

b) The Hunger Games.   **d)** The Maze Runner.

- ( ) Waking up with no memories and in a strange place surrounded by a lethal maze, he becomes obsessed with finding a way out there.

- ( ) Annually, twelve districts are forced to randomly choose a girl and a boy to fight till death in a game on live television.

- ( ) After being accused of stealing Zeus' lightning bolt, he embarks on an adventure to catch the true thief, save his mom, and unravel a powerful mystery.

- ( ) After her best friend Roger disappears, she sets out with her daemon on an epic quest to rescue him and save her world.

4 In which one would you like to be? What would you do there?

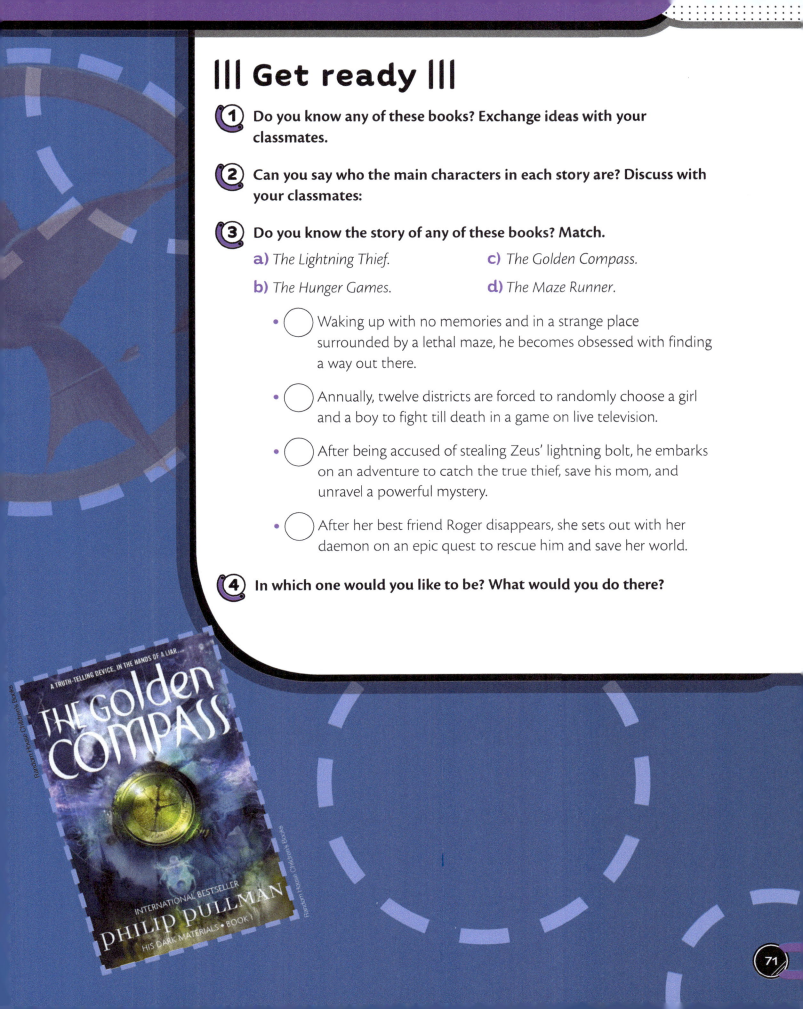

Let's practice

1. What kind of stories are they reading?

adventure • detective • fairy tale • fantasy • horror / thriller • sci-fi

a)
_____

d)
_____

b)
_____

e)
_____

c)
_____

f)
_____

2. Reorder the letters to find out what kind of text it is.

a) EPROTY _____

b) YBHIPOAGR _____

c) NIFICOT _____

d) WENS _____

e) YLPA _____

f) LIHAICSOTR _____

3 **Look at this scene and answer the questions.**

a) Where was he?
_____

b) How many birthday cards were there?
_____

c) How many owls were there?
_____

d) How many lamps were there?
_____

4 **Look at the previous image and complete the sentences using was, was not, were or were not.**

a) Harry _____ happy.

b) His suitcase _____ closed.

c) His book _____ on the floor.

d) An envelope _____ on his bed.

e) Both lamps _____ switched on.

f) The owls _____ asleep.

g) There _____ many books in his bedroom.

h) His birthday cards _____ on his table.

5 **Complete the questions using was or were.**

a) _____ it a birthday party?

b) Where _____ his friends?

c) _____ he alone?

d) _____ his friends hiding?

e) _____ the dogs outside?

f) _____ Bob at school yesterday?

LANGUAGE PIECE

Simple past: to be

Affirmative
I / He / She / It – was
We / You / They – were

Negative
I / He / She / It – was not / wasn't
We / You / They – were not / weren't

Interrogative
Was – I / He / She / It
Were – We / You / They

Let's listen n' speak

1. Listen to the synopsis of the book *The Expeditioners and the Treasure of Drowned Man's Canyon* and then answer the questions.

a) What did people use to think?
- ◯ There were only seven continents and five oceans.
- ◯ There weren't more than seven continents and five oceans.

b) What happened? _____

c) What did people find out?
- ◯ Maps were a lie.
- ◯ Maps were not a lie.
- ◯ There were more places in the world.
- ◯ There were fewer places in the world.

d) What did the kids' father help to do?

_____

e) What happened to the kids' father? _____

f) How will they decipher the mystery?
- ◯ By analyzing the map.
- ◯ By encoding the map.

g) What are the kids' abilities?
- ◯ Be brave.
- ◯ Crack codes.
- ◯ Be fearful.
- ◯ Fix things.
- ◯ Break things.
- ◯ Make codes.

h) What did their father leave them? _____

i) What expedition was it related to?
- ◯ Amazon Desert.
- ◯ Anthem Desert.
- ◯ Arizona Desert.
- ◯ Aurea Desert.

j) Who wants to get there first? _____

Let's practice

1) Read the synopsis of the book *The Expeditioners and the Secret of King Triton's Lair* and then answer the questions.

MOVIES

The Expeditioners

After their escapade in *Drowned Man's Canyon*, Kit, Zander, M.K. West and Sukey were back in another adventure! The Wests joined the Academy for the Exploratory Sciences, a school for expeditioners.

Kit **encountered** a mysterious map left by their father with clues that **lead** to an island in the North Caribbean. It's the perfect excuse to go there.

The Academy had a yearly program that **allowed** the students to make a request to go on an expedition of their choice. But when their rival at the Academy, Lazlo Nackley, **stole** their idea and got chosen to become head of the operation, it all started **to go downhill**.

Lazlo's evil, controlling father came along as a **chaperone** for the Wests, and Sukey **knew** that they had a hard journey coming on, but there was much more they weren't expecting.

GLOSSARY

Allowed (to allow): permitiu (permitir).
Chaperone: acompanhante.
Encountered (to encounter): encontrou (encontrar).
Knew (to know): sabia (saber).
Lead (to lead): conduz (conduzir).
Stole (to steal): roubou (roubar).
To go downhill: dar errado.

a) Which Academy did the kids join after their escapade in *Drowned Man's Canyon*?

- ◯ Expeditioners Sciences.
- ◯ Exploratory Sciences.
- ◯ Exploratory Seas.

b) What did Kit encounter? _____

c) Where does this map lead? _____

d) Write **T** (true) or **F** (false).

- ◯ The Wests and Sukey joined an expedition.
- ◯ Kit was the head of the operation.
- ◯ Lazlo Nackley was their friend.
- ◯ Lazlo's father was the chaperone in the expedition.
- ◯ The expedition was a success.

2 These are the verbs from the text. Tick all that are in the past tense.

a) ◯ allowed
b) ◯ came
c) ◯ coming on
d) ◯ encountered
e) ◯ got chosen
f) ◯ joined
g) ◯ lead
h) ◯ left
i) ◯ to become
j) ◯ started
k) ◯ stole
l) ◯ to go
m) ◯ to make
n) ◯ were

> **LANGUAGE PIECE**
>
> **Simple past: regular verbs**
>
> Ending with (**-e**):
>   believ**e** → believ**ed**.
>
> Ending with (**-y**) and preceded by a consonant: tr**y** → tr**ied**.
>
> Ending with (**-y**) preceded by a vowel: pla**y** → pla**yed**.
>
> Ending in **CVC**: s**top** → s**topped**.
>
> The rest of the verbs:
>   watch → watch**ed**.

3 Write the simple past form of the following verbs.

a) add _____
b) answer _____
c) beg _____
d) brush _____
e) call _____
f) cry _____
g) discover _____
h) exist _____
i) watch _____
j) stop _____

> **LANGUAGE PIECE**
>
> **Simple past: affirmative sentences**
>
> Subject pronoun + verb (simple past) + complement
>
> I **listened** to the radio yesterday.

4 Unscramble the words to make sentences. Use the verbs in the simple past form.

a) last / to / weekend / she / the / **travel** / beach
_____

b) basketball / I / Saturday / **play** / on
_____

c) friends / **travel** / to Europe / my / last vacation / on their
_____

d) seventeen / **move** / when / she / to São Paulo / Maria / **be**
_____

e) how / Dean / in / **learn** / to ice skate / Canada
_____

5. Rewrite the sentences using the negative form of the simple past.

a) George listened to music yesterday.

_____

b) It rained a lot in our city in July.

_____

c) I tried Japanese food last night.

_____

LANGUAGE PIECE

Simple past: affirmative sentences

Subject pronoun + auxiliary verb (did) + not + verb (infinitive) + complement

I did not listen to the radio yesterday.

6. Write questions for the following answers.

a) _____

Yes, Leo studied Spanish last semester.

b) _____

No, I didn't watch TV last night.

c) _____

Yes, Brian lived in the USA.

LANGUAGE PIECE

Simple past: interrogative sentences

Auxiliary verb (did) + subject pronoun + verb (infinitive) + complement

Did you listen to the radio yesterday?

7. Find and circle the mistakes and rewrite the sentence.

a) I relax on the beach last summer.

_____

_____

b) Do you liked the movie last night?

_____

_____

c) Yes, I did use my computer this morning.

_____

d) You cleaned your bedroom?

_____

e) He didn't climbed trees when he was a boy.

_____

TRACK 14

Vocabulary hint

There are three forms of pronouncing the past of regular verbs:

Unvoiced consonants: pronounced like (-**t**).

Look → Loo**k**ed

Voiced consonants: pronounced like (-**d**).

Save → Sa**ve**d

Vowel sound: pronounced like (**d**).

Stay → Sta**y**ed

Let's listen n' speak

1 **Listen to Edward and Clint's conversation and answer the following questions.**

a) What did Edward do in the morning?
_____

b) How did Edward get to the library?
_____

c) What did Edward and his mom do after they decided to go home?
_____

d) What did Edward and his girlfriend do that day?
_____

2 **Organize Edward's day timeline according to what you heard.**

a) ◯ Walked to the library.
b) ◯ Started reading a book.
c) ◯ Stopped at the new restaurant.
d) ◯ Needed to go to her house.
e) ◯ Studied from 8:00 to 11:00.

f) ◯ Visited her aunt.
g) ◯ His mom arrived.
h) ◯ His girlfriend called.
i) ◯ Decided to go home.
j) ◯ Remembered his homework.

3 **Rewrite the sentences according to the instruction.**

a) Edward visited his girlfriend's aunt. (negative)
_____

b) Edward didn't read a biography at the library. (interrogative)
_____

c) Did Edward stop at the new restaurant with his mom? (affirmative)
_____

4 **Work in pairs and role-play Edward and Clint's dialogue.**

Let's read n' write

1 Read the beginning of *Gulliver's Travels* to find out more about his adventures and answer the questions.

Gulliver's Travels

One stormy night at sea, a ship was **wrecked**. All the passengers on board **drowned**, except Lemuel Gulliver. Gulliver was an excellent swimmer and swam for many miles before he **reached** shore. Gulliver was very tired and decided to sleep. He would look for food after he had had sufficient rest.

Gulliver slept for a whole day. When he woke up, the Sun was **beating down** upon him. He tried to move, he could not. His hair, hands, legs and body were tied to the ground. He saw little men running all around him. Someone had got a tiny ladder and was **climbing up** to him. The little man, no bigger than Gulliver's thumbnail, came up to his ears and said, "You are in the land of Lilliput; we are Lilliputians. We are taking you to our Emperor, so please do not make any trouble. You will be shot at." Gulliver almost laughed at this **threat** but **nodded**. [...]

Available at: <www.kidsgen.com/stories/classic_stories/gullivers_travels.htm#2Vrmx8t8T0v2edrC.99>. Access: July 2018.

GLOSSARY

Beating down (to beat down): brilhando (brilhar) intensamente.

Climbing up (to climb up): escalando (escalar).

Drowned (to drown): afogou (afogar).

Nodded (to nod): acenou (acenar) com a cabeça.

Reached (to reach): alcançou (alcançar).

Threat (to threat): ameaça; ameaçar.

Wrecked (to wreck): naufragou, afundou (naufragar, afundar).

a) What is the text about?

_____

b) What happened to Gulliver? Write if it is **T** (true) or **F** (false).

- ◯ Gulliver's ship wrecked.
- ◯ Gulliver's ship reached the shore.
- ◯ Gulliver's crew died.
- ◯ Gulliver's crew almost drowned.

c) How did Gulliver survive?

_____

d) What did he do when he reached the shore?

_____

e) What happened when Gulliver woke up?

_____

f) Who did he meet there?

- ◯ The Lillitupians.
- ◯ The Lilliputians.
- ◯ The Lillibutians.

g) How tall were the Lilliputians?

_____

2) What is the genre of this text?

_____

3) Check all the characteristics of this kind of text.

- **a)** ◯ arguments
- **b)** ◯ classification
- **c)** ◯ commentary
- **d)** ◯ description
- **e)** ◯ information
- **f)** ◯ list
- **g)** ◯ main character
- **h)** ◯ plot
- **i)** ◯ rhyme
- **j)** ◯ sequence
- **k)** ◯ setting
- **l)** ◯ visual aids

4) What is the theme of this story?

- **a)** ◯ Epic.
- **b)** ◯ Adventure.
- **c)** ◯ Fairy tale.
- **d)** ◯ Humor.
- **e)** ◯ Poetry.
- **f)** ◯ Biography.

It is your turn. Get ready to write a short story of your own. Check the following tips before you start.

Plan before you begin

1. Decide on a scenario.
2. Develop characters.
3. Choose a point of view.
4. Use setting and context.
5. Set up a plot.
6. Create conflict and tension.
7. Build to a crisis or climax.
8. Find a solution.
9. Write a draft.
10. Revise your essay.

Based on: <www.wikihow.com/Write-a-Narrative-Essay>. Access: July 2018.

Now, read the following prompts, follow your teacher's instructions and use your imagination

Fairies in Danger
Imagine you are a fairy living in a beautiful forest. One day you heard a loud rumbling noise so you headed towards it to investigate. You saw a strange yellow machine with many wheels and a large iron shovel that can dig up the earth and knock down trees. You overheard people saying they were going to clear the forest with this machine and build a shopping mall. You rushed back to the fairy village to warn the other fairies…

Secret Passage in an Egyptian Pyramid
Your class took a field trip to Egypt to learn about the ancient Egyptians. You traveled to the Pyramids at Giza. It was a hot, sunny day when the bus arrived there. Your classmates went into the pyramid with a tour guide who showed the passages and explained its history. You had a book on hieroglyphics and found an interesting picture that said, 'Press here'…

The Evil Villain
Evil laughter rang out. You knew something was amiss. You turned around and there he stood, grinning his wicked smile. "You have eaten my poison. It will kill you within a day unless you take this antidote which only I have. However, if you do something for me, I will give you the antidote. What I want you to do…"

The Tunnel in the Forest
Your parents sent you to Canada to study English. You don't know anyone and there was nothing to do. You sat in the park at the edge of the forest. Then you looked into the forest. Your teacher warned you to stay in the park but you were curious so you walked through the trees. After a short while you found a secret tunnel…

What story will you choose? Why?

CHAPTER 4

||| Citizenship moment |||

SEPTEMBER 8

LITERACY IS A HUMAN RIGHT

"Literacy for all is at the heart of basic education for all... [and] creating literate environments and societies is essential for achieving the goals or eradicating poverty, reducing child mortality, curbing population growth, achieving gender equality and ensuring sustainable development, peace and democracy." (UNESCO, 2002)

Cristiane Viana

INTERNATIONAL LITERACY DAY

750 MILLION PEOPLE WORLDWIDE CANNOT READ OR WRITE

About 10% OF THE WORLD'S POPULATION ARE ILLITERATE

TWO-THIRDS of all illiterate people are **women**

"Every literate woman is a victory over poverty."
Ban Ki-moon.

27% of all illiterate adults live in sub-Saharan Africa

49% of the global illiterate population is found in Southern Asia

More than 90% of all non-literates live in developing countries

WHAT KEEPS CHILDREN AND YOUTH OUT OF SCHOOL?

CHILD LABOR is a major factor keeping children out of school. Around 150 million children are involved in labor.

POVERTY is other major factor keeping children out of school. No money for school, fees and uniforms is an obstacle.

ILLITERATE PARENTS often place less value in the education of their children. The lack of parental support affects the children negatively.

LACKING INFRASTRUCTURE difficult access to school.

GLOSSARY

Curbing (to curb): refreando (refrear).
Fees: taxas.
Goals: metas.
Illiterate: analfabeto(a).
Literate: alfabetizado(a).
Place (to place): colocam (colocar).
Poverty: pobreza.
Sustainable: sustentável.
Two-thirds: dois terços.

Based on: *Literacy among youth is rising, but young women lag behind*, available at: <https://data.unicef.org/topic/education/literacy/>; *International Literacy Day*, available at: <http://uis.unesco.org/en/news/international-literacy-day-2017>. *World Top 20 Projects*, available at: <https://worldtop20.org/illiteracy-rates>. Access: July 2018.

1. **Check all that apply to explain why literacy is a human right.**

   a) ◯ Crucial for eradicating poverty.
   b) ◯ Crucial for keeping poverty.
   c) ◯ Gender fairness.
   d) ◯ Gender imbalance.
   e) ◯ Reduces child mortality.
   f) ◯ Restricts population growth.
   g) ◯ The core part of basic education.
   h) ◯ The least important part of basic education.
   i) ◯ Viable development.
   j) ◯ Wasteful development.

2. **What does it mean to be an illiterate person?**

   _____
   _____

3. **What is the percentage of illiterate people in the world?**

   _____
   _____

4. **Are there more female or male illiterate people?**

   _____
   _____

5. **Where can the majority of global illiterate adults be found? What is the percentage?**

   _____
   _____

6. **What are the reasons that keep children and youth out of school?**

   _____
   _____

PROJECT

Fight Illiteracy

How about joining efforts to spread the reading culture in your neighborhood?

Team up with your classmates and develop a project to boost the reading practices within your community. Brainstorm ideas about ways to make their access to books easier and find out with your teacher which one is more likely to be done for you!

EXPLORING

Reading is Fundamental (RIF)
- www.rif.org

UNESCO
- http://en.unesco.org/themes/literacy

Project Literacy
- www.projectliteracy.com/partners/center-literacy

UNIT 6
DID YOU SEE THIS MOVIE?

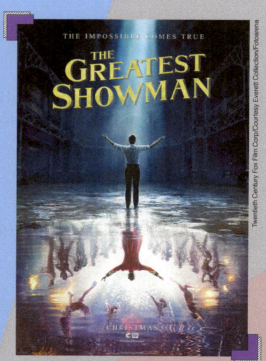

||| Get ready |||

1 Observe the pictures. What do they have in common?
_____

2 Have you ever watched any of them? Talk a little bit about it.

3 Some movies are represented by different music styles. Write down the music style you think best describes the following movie genres.

a) drama _____   c) action _____

b) comedy _____   d) thriller _____

4 Talk to your friends.

a) Do you like cinema?

b) What is your favorite movie style? Why?

c) What are the characteristics of your favorite movie style?

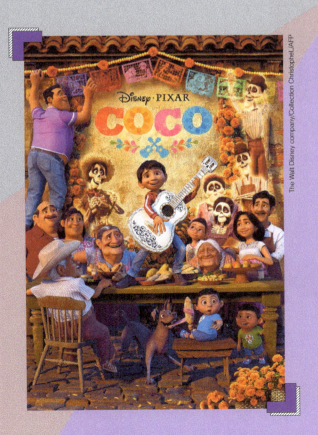
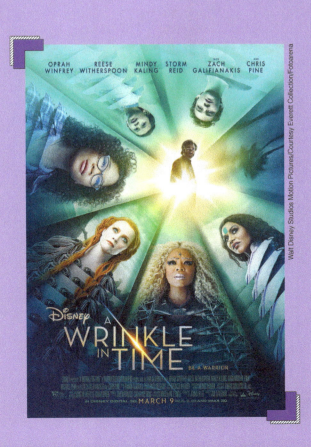

CHAPTER 1

Let's practice

1) Unscramble the letters and find out some movie genres.

a) RAW _____

b) MALUICS _____

c) LOPAITCIL _____

d) ESWNERT _____

2) Fill in the gaps with the correct movie genre based on the context of the enunciation.

> action • adventure • comedy • historical • sci-fi

a) A movie that makes you laugh is a _____.

b) A movie that is exciting with lots of guns and explosions is an _____ movie.

c) Movies about the future or space are known as _____ films.

d) A movie about real life events is a _____ movie.

e) A film about lots of travelling and exciting dangerous events is an _____.

3) Can you name the genre of the following movies?

a)
Tell Them We Are Rising: The Story of Black Colleges and Universities

_____

c)
Annabelle: Creation

_____

> documentary
> drama
> horror
> saga

b)
Wonder

_____

d)
Pirates of the Caribbean: Dead men tell no tales

_____

4) What are these artists' musical styles?

> classical • country • heavy metal • jazz
> pop • rap • reggae • rock • samba

a) Kiss

_____

d) Blake Shelton

_____

g) Nat King Cole

_____

b) Kanye West

_____

e) Metallica

_____

h) Bob Marley

_____

c) Mozart

_____

f) Rihanna

_____

i) Cartola

_____

5) Complete the name of the following instruments.

a) D _____ u _____ s

b) _____ u _____ ta _____

c) Fl _____ t _____

d) _____ io _____ in

e) Pi _____ n _____

f) _____ a _____ oph _____ n _____

1 Listen about the movies on exhibition and complete the texts with the missing information.

MOVIES TIMES

Today
AMC 84TH STREET 6
MISSION: IMPOSSIBLE - FALLOUT

_____ / Adventure /
_____

    Ethan Hunt and his IMF team, along with some familiar **allies**, race against time after a mission gone wrong.

ANT-MAN AND THE WASP

_____ / Adventure /
_____ / Fantasy

    As Scott Lang balances being both a Super Hero and a father, Hope van Dyne and Dr. Hank Pym present an urgent new mission that finds the Ant-Man fighting **alongside** The Wasp to **uncover** secrets from their past.

CITY CINEMAS EAST
86TH STREET

HOTEL TRANSYLVANIA 3: SUMMER VACATION

_____ / Adventure /
_____ / Action

    Count Dracula and company participate in a cruise for sea-loving monsters, **unaware** that their boat is being **commandeered** by the monster-hating Van Helsing family.

MAMMA MIA! HERE WE GO AGAIN

Music / _____

    Five years after the events of Mamma Mia!, Sophie learns about her mother's past while **pregnant** herself.

GLOSSARY

Allies: aliados(as).
Alongside: ao lado de.
Commandeered (to commandeer): comandado (comandar).
Pregnant: grávida.
Unaware: sem ter conhecimento, sem saber.
Uncover: descobrir.
Wasp: vespa.

2 Now, answer:

a) Which movie is an animated cartoon? _____

b) Which one probably involved espionage? _____

c) In which one is the main character a superhero? _____

d) Which one is a musical? _____

3 Team up and discuss the following topics.

• What is your favorite kind of movies?
• Where do you prefer to watch movies? Why?

Let's practice

1 Read this musical review and answer the questions.

■ **THEATER PLAYBILL**

Matilda The Musical

BROADWAY | MUSICAL | ORIGINAL   Sam S. Shubert Theatre

Synopsis

Based on the **beloved** novel by best--selling author Roald Dahl, *Matilda* is the story of an extraordinary girl who dreams of a better life. Unloved by her parents but with a special bond developed with her schoolteacher, *Matilda* dares **to take a stand** and change her destiny armed only with a vivid imagination, a **sharp** mind, and **psychokinetic** powers.

Based on: <www.playbill.com/events/event_detail/matilda-at-sam-s.-shubert-theatre-63952>. Access: July 2018.

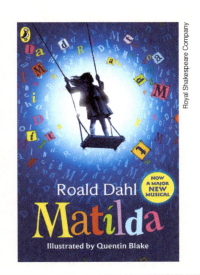
Royal Shakespeare Company

GLOSSARY

Beloved: amado(a).

Psychokinetic: telecinético(a).

Sharp: aguçada(o); afiada(o).

To take a stand: posicionar-se, fazer uma escolha.

a) What is the review about: a movie or a musical play? How do you know it?

_____

_____

b) Check all the characteristics listed to describe Matilda.

- ◯ agile mind
- ◯ boring imagination
- ◯ bright imagination
- ◯ kinesthetic powers
- ◯ little girl
- ◯ psychokinetic powers

c) What personal problems did Matilda have? _____

2 On your notebook, copy and complete the following table with the verbs from the text.

verb	verb tense	infinitive form	simple past form

3 Rewrite the previous text using only the simple past tense.

■ **THEATER PLAYBILL**

Matilda The Musical

BROADWAY | MUSICAL | ORIGINAL   Sam S. Shubert Theatre

Synopsis

_____

_____

_____

_____

_____

_____

4 Look at the past tense of the following verbs and tell if they are **R** (regular) or **I** (irregular).

a) ◯ were
b) ◯ dreamed
c) ◯ took
d) ◯ changed
e) ◯ had
f) ◯ impressed
g) ◯ saw
h) ◯ felt
i) ◯ learned

LANGUAGE PIECE

Simple past: irregular verbs
In English there are some verbs with different past forms, they are called irregular verbs because there is no rule for their past tense. Check the Language Court to see a list of them.

5 Read the following verbs closely and put them in the correct column.

base form	simple past form	base form	simple past form
meet		eat	
	forgot		read
	had		lost

ate
forget
have
lose
met
read

6 Say if they are regular R (regular) or I (irregular) and write their simple past form.

a) ( ) fly _____
b) ( ) use _____
c) ( ) study _____
d) ( ) eat _____
e) ( ) make _____
f) ( ) travel _____
g) ( ) see _____
h) ( ) sleep _____

7 Rewrite the following sentences in the simple past.

a) **I understand** everything when **I read** travel books.

_____

b) Jane **doesn't write** a post card to me.

_____

c) **Does** Alice **help** her mother with the shopping list?

_____

d) Jake **goes** to safaris when he **travels** with his dad.

_____

e) Elizabeth and Jane **don't bring** us any souvenir from France.

_____

8 Complete the short conversations.

a) A: _____ you _____ anything special over the weekend? (do)

B: Yes, I _____. I _____ to the mountains and _____ hiking with Lea. (drive – go)

b) A: Why _____ you _____ Victor but not me? (call)

B: Sorry, I _____ your phone number. I _____ my notebook at home. (forget – leave)

Vocabulary hint
Vowel sounds

beat	boot
bit	book
bait	boat
bet	bought
bat	box
but	by
sofa	cow
her	boy

TRACK 17

91

Let's listen n' speak

1 Listen to Margo and Jane and complete the dialogue with the missing verbs.

Jane: Hi, Margo! What's up?

Margo: Hey, Jane. I _____ to the movies with my mom.

Jane: Cool! Which movie did you _____?

Margo: We _____ Leap!

Jane: I didn't _____ this movie yet. What _____ it about?

Margo: It _____ about an 11-year-old girl named Félicie. Her mom _____ to leave her on orphanage steps when she was a baby. She _____ of becoming a famous ballerina.

Jane: Wow! It _____ to be a nice story!

Margo: And it is. I _____ it lot.

Jane: What else _____ in the movie?

Margo: Hum… Well, Félicie's best friend _____ Victor, who was a talented young inventor. They _____ away together from the orphanage to go to Paris.

Jane: Wow! Really? Did they _____ into much trouble?

Margo: Yes, they _____. But I'm not telling you.

Jane: Ok, fine! Just _____ me one more thing. Did they _____ a happy ending?

Margo: You can _____ on that, Jane. Mom is calling. It is dinner time. See you tomorrow.

Jane: See you.

2 Listen to the dialogue again and mark the true statements with an X.

a) ◯ Jane already watched the movie Leap!

b) ◯ Félicie was a very good dancer who wanted to be a ballerina.

c) ◯ Victor was a very talented inventor.

Let's read n' write

1) Read the following movie review and answer the questions.

Available at: <www.imdb.com/title/tt1856101/?ref_=fn_al_tt_1>. Access: July 2018.

a) What is the story about?

_____

_____

_____

b) What do you think it happened in the movie?

_____

_____

_____

GLOSSARY

Been missing (to be missing): está (estar) desaparecido(a).

Discovery: descoberta.

Former: antigo(a).

Leads (to lead): conduz, leva (conduzir, levar).

Long-buried: há muito enterrado(a).

Quest: busca.

To plunge: mergulhar.

To track down: rastrear.

Unearths (to unearth): desenterra (desenterrar).

c) What kind of text is it?

- ◯ Article.
- ◯ Narrative.
- ◯ Summary.
- ◯ Instructions.
- ◯ News.
- ◯ Review.

d) What is the movie genre according to this review?

- ◯ Action.
- ◯ Comedy.
- ◯ Mystery.
- ◯ Sci-Fi.
- ◯ Drama.
- ◯ Thriller.

e) Check all the information you can find in the text.

- ◯ title
- ◯ genre
- ◯ plot
- ◯ set
- ◯ period in time
- ◯ actors
- ◯ spoilers
- ◯ writers
- ◯ viewers opinions
- ◯ duration
- ◯ release date
- ◯ characters description
- ◯ viewers rate
- ◯ story narrative
- ◯ details on the making

2 Thinking about the movie review you read, complete the following chart.

	Adjective to describe it
Title	great boring interesting amusing surprising horrible not very good excellent etc.
	Characteristics
Genre	songs / music mystery love / romance surprises ghosts /spirits futuristic events laughter/ fun special effects danger etc.
The plot	

3. Think about a movie you already saw and that you liked. Gather the following pieces of information about it and complete the table.

Title	Adjective to describe it
Genre	**Characteristics**
The plot	

4. Write the review of two movies you chose previously.

5. Now, on your notebook, write your opinion about the movie. Talk about its characteristics, what was more interesting, soundtrack, plot, genre etc.

Chapter 4

||| Tying in |||

Everybody loves some good music, right? It helps you relax, celebrate, think, exercise and even study. But music is not only for entertaining. Music can also change the world. That's what people from the project *Playing for Change* believe. Have you ever heard of it? No? So now you have:

> **GLOSSARY**
> **Agreed (to agree):** concordou (concordar).
> **Boundaries:** fronteiras.
> **Co-founders:** cofundadores.
> **Heartbeat:** batida do coração.
> **Inspire:** inspirar.
> **Nonprofit organization:** organização não governamental.

Playing for change

The Journey

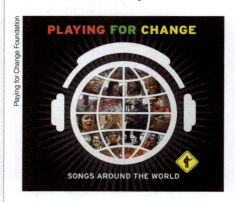

Playing for Change Foundation

Playing For Change is a movement created to **inspire** and connect the world through music. The idea for this project came from a common belief that music has the power to break down **boundaries** and overcome distances between people.

Playing For Change was born in 2002 as a shared vision between **co-founders**, Mark Johnson and Whitney Kroenke, to hit the streets of America with a mobile recording studio and cameras in search of inspiration and the **heartbeat** of the people. This musical journey resulted in the award-winning documentary, "A Cinematic Discovery of Street Musicians."

In 2005, Mark Johnson was walking in Santa Monica, California, when he heard the voice of Roger Ridley singing "Stand By Me." Roger had so much soul and conviction in his voice, and Mark approached him about performing "Stand By Me" as a Song Around the World. Roger **agreed**, and when Mark returned with recording equipment and cameras he asked Roger, "With a voice like yours, why are you singing on the streets?" Roger replied, "Man I'm in the Joy business, I come out to be with the people." Ever since that day the Playing For Change crew has traveled the world recording and filming musicians, creating Songs Around the World, and building a global family.

Creating Songs Around the World inspired us to unite many of the greatest musicians we met throughout our journey in the creation of the Playing For Change Band. These musicians come from many different countries and cultures, but through music they speak the same language. Songs Around The World The PFC Band is now touring the world and spreading the message of love and hope to audiences everywhere.

The true measure of any movement is what it gives back to the people. We therefore created the Playing For Change Foundation, a separate 501(c)3 **nonprofit organization** dedicated to building music and art schools for children around the world, and creating hope and inspiration for the future of our planet.

No matter who you are or where you come from, we are all united through music. [...]

Playing for Change. Available at: <http://playingforchange.com/about/>. Access: July 2018.

Let's practice

1. What is the idea that inspired the project?

   _____
   _____
   _____

2. What is the central message the founders want to show with the Playing for Change Band?

   _____
   _____
   _____

3. As you have read, Playing for Change is a project to help change the world through music. Do you know any other project like that in Brazil?

   _____
   _____
   _____

EXPLORING

Stand by Me
- www.youtube.com/watch?v=oiPzU75P9FA&list=PL5we5wdVumpqOtUzGpp27dEDnMvy0dtuA

Projetos de música
- www.projetoguri.org.br/

PROJECT

Brazilian Popular Songs

Research to answer the questions:
- What are the most popular types of music in Brazil?
- What are the most popular musical instruments in our country?
- Are there any typical instruments from Brazil?

Make posters relating these answers to exhibit around the classroom.

Music video

As an extra project, choose a famous song in English that you believe to have an important message to the world. Record a video of you and your friends playing it and share this video with the school community.

REVIEW

1 What kind of movie is it? Mark the best option.

a)

- ○ Fairy Tale.
- ○ Thriller.
- ○ Animation.

c)

- ○ Detective.
- ○ Sci-fi.
- ○ Adventure.

b)

- ○ Fantasy.
- ○ Detective.
- ○ Biography.

d)

- ○ Fairy Tale.
- ○ Romance.
- ○ War.

2 Complete with **was** or **were**.

a) _____ your sister at school yesterday?

b) How many apples _____ there on the table this morning?

c) How _____ your friends after the problem?

d) _____ I late yesterday? I don't remember!

3 Complete the gaps and the crossword puzzle below with the simple past tense of the following verbs.

ACROSS

2. to start _____

5. to make _____

7. to go _____

8. to come _____

DOWN

1. to become _____

3. to allow _____

4. to leave _____

6. to have _____

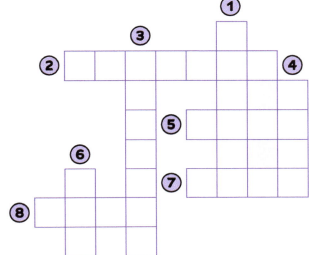

4 Write questions for the following answers.

a) _____
I went to the movies yesterday.

b) _____
The class started at 7:30 this morning.

c) _____
Yes, we watched the horror movie last night.

d) _____
No, I didn't like the food.

e) _____
I saw a very scary movie yesterday.

DO NOT FORGET!

SIMPLE PAST TENSE

Verb to be
Irregular

I was	I wasn't	Was I?
You were	You weren't	Were you?
He was	He wasn't	Was he?
She was	She wasn't	Was she?
It was	It wasn't	Was it?
We were	We weren't	Were we?
You were	You weren't	Were you?
They were	They weren't	Were they?

Irregular verbs
No specific rule

Examples:
- TO DO → DID
- TO HAVE → HAD
- TO GO → WENT
- TO BUY → BOUGHT

Regular verbs
Verb + ED

Examples:
- TO LOVE → LOVED
- TO START → STARTED
- TO STUDY → STUDIED
- TO WORK → WORKED

SIMPLE PAST TENSE SENTENCE CONSTRUCTION

AFFIRMATIVE: Subject + verb (past tense) + complement.
EXAMPLE: Arthur visited his grandparents yesterday.

NEGATIVE: Subject + did + not + verb (infinitive without to) + complement.
EXAMPLE: Arthur did not (didn't) visit his grandparents yesterday.

INTERROGATIVE: Did + subject + verb (infinitive without to) + complement?
EXAMPLE: Did Arthur visit his grandparents yesterday?

IMPORTANT WORDS: Title genre – plot – writer.

KINDS OF TEXTS
- poetry
- biography
- fiction
- news
- play
- musical

KINDS OF STORIES
- adventure
- detective
- fairy tale
- fantasy
- horror / thriller
- sci-fi

KINDS OF MOVIES
- war
- romance
- animation
- drama
- musical
- comedy

KINDS OF MUSIC
- country
- pop
- reggae
- jazz
- rock
- samba

IMPORTANT WORDS: actors – set – spoiler – duration.

IMPORTANT WORDS: band – hit – album – singer.

OVERCOMING CHALLENGES

(EEAR – 2016)

Read the text and answer the question.

The story of a blind girl

There was a blind girl who hated herself just because she <u>was</u> blind. She hated everyone, except her loving boyfriend. He was always there for her. She <u>said</u> that if she could only see the world, she would marry her boyfriend.

One day, someone <u>donated</u> a pair of eyes to her and then she could see everything, including her boyfriend. Her boyfriend asked her, "Now that you can see the world, will you marry me?"

The girl was shocked when she saw that her boyfriend was blind too, and <u>refused</u> to marry him. Her boyfriend <u>walked</u> away in tears, and later <u>wrote</u> a letter to her saying: "Just take care of my eyes dear."

The underlined verbs in the text are in the:

a) Simple Past.   **b)** Simple Present.   **c)** Present Perfect.   **d)** Present Continuous.

(PUC-GO – 2016)

In Text 8, most of the verbs in Portuguese are conjugated in the past tense, such as "*chegou*", "*enamorou-se*" e *resistiu*". Complete the following text using the correct past tense conjugation of the verbs in parenthesis in English:

Last night Susan (go) _____ to her friend's birthday party. She (dance) _____ with her boyfriend, and (eat) _____ cake. After they (leave) _____ the party, Susan and her boyfriend (decide) _____ to go and watch a movie at the theater. They (see) _____ the new Transformer's movie, and then they went home. When she (get) _____ home, Susan (take) _____ a shower and (fall) _____ asleep quickly.

Choose the correct option from the ones listed below:

a) Go / dance / eat / leave / decide / see / get / take / fall.

b) Went / danced / ate / left / decided / saw / got / took / fell.

c) Will go / will dance / will eat / will leave / will decide / will see / will get / will take / will fall.

d) Had gone / had danced / had eaten / had left / had decided / had seen / had gotten / had taken / had fallen.

UNIT 7
WHAT DO THEY LOOK LIKE?

Margo Gru

Felonius Gru   Lucy Wilde   Edith Gru   Agnes Gru

Marlena Gru

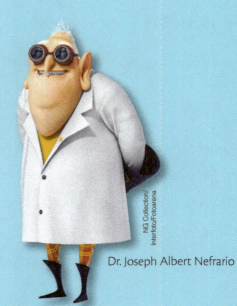
Dr. Joseph Albert Nefrario

||| Get ready |||

1 Do you know these characters? Where do you know them from? Talk to your classmates.

2 Do they have the same physical characteristics or are they different?

_____

3 Who looks like this? Write the character's name under the physical characteristic he/she presents.

Physical characteristic	Character	Physical characteristic	Character
tall		brunette	
short		blonde	
bald		red hair	
chubby/fat		gray hair	
thin/slim		blue eyes	
glasses		green eyes	
brown hair		brown eyes	
wart		dark/black eyes	

103

Let's practice

1 Match the description with the correct image.

a)  b)  c)

- ( ) Sara is chubby and short. She has curly hair and wears glasses.
- ( ) Polly is tall and thin. She has dark hair.
- ( ) Peter is tall and old. He is bald and has a white beard.

2 Organize the words into the correct categories.

bald • blond • blue • brown
chubby • red • slim • thin

Eyes	Hair	Weight

3 Choose the best option according to the picture.

a)  b)

My teeth are _____. My doctor has a _____.

- ( ) small • ( ) big   • ( ) mustache • ( ) beard

104

4) What do they look like? Follow the example.

a)  He is about 12 years old, he is quite chubby. He has blue eyes, red hair and wears braces.

c)

b)

d)

5) Complete these wanted people posters.

WANTED

Wanted for Blizzard
Queen Elsa from Arandelle

Age 21

_____ skin, blue _____,

_____, _____ hair.

WANTED

Wanted for church
Quasimodo

Age 20

_____ skin, blue _____,

_____ hair and a _____.

Let's listen n' speak

1. Listen to a chat between Justin and Paul. Answer the questions.

a) What are Justin and Paul talking about?

_____

b) What does the girl look like?

_____

c) Which adjective describes personality? _____

d) Which sentence is used to ask about the girl?

- ◯ Who is she? Is she beautiful?
- ◯ Who she is? She is beautiful?

e) What does she look like? Circle the most suitable image.

2. Who is this person? Choose a caricature below and describe him or her to the opposite team.

a)
Cristiano Ronaldo.

c)
Letitia Wright.

e)
Elle Fanning.

b)
Daisy Ridley.

d)
Jimi Hendrix.

f)
Gaten Matarazzo.

CHAPTER 2

Let's practice

1) Write questions for the given answers.

a) _____
He's handsome, short and has brown hair.

b) _____
They are cute and have red hair.

c) _____
No, Lucy is very tall.

d) _____
No, she doesn't. She has blue eyes.

LANGUAGE PIECE
- What do/does (person) look like?
- (person) is *tall / short / cute / chubby* etc.
- Do / Does (person) have (characteristic)?
- Yes, (person) *do / does*.
- No, (person) *don't / doesn't*.

2) Read Maggie's description chart and answer the questions.

Name	Maggie	Height	medium
Surname	Peterson	Weight	slim
Age	12	Likes	read, draw and write
Lives with	parents and little sister	Favorite pet	dog
Hair color	red	Biggest quality	friendly
Eye color	dark brown	Biggest weakness	talkative

a) How old is Maggie?
_____

b) What color is her hair?
_____

c) What color are her eyes?
_____

d) What is her height?
_____

e) Is she chubby or thin?
_____

f) What is her best quality and her biggest weakness?
_____
_____

107

3) Match the adjectives below to their correct descriptions.

a) hesitant **b)** reliable **c)** generous **d)** selfish

- (b) Someone who can be trusted to do something well.
- (c) Someone who is willing to give money or help freely.
- (d) Someone who thinks of their own advantage.
- (a) Someone who is slow to act because they feel uncertain.

4) Put the adjectives from the box in the correct column.

absent-minded • cheerful • clumsy • easy-going • generous
hesitant • jealous • lazy • neat • quiet • reliable • selfish

Positive	Negative
cheerful	absent-minded
easy-going	clumsy
generous	hesitant
neat	jealous
quiet	lazy
reliable	selfish

5) Use the words from the box to complete the definitions below.

cheerful • hard-working • pessimistic • rude • tidy

a) Jane is the most ____cheerful____ person I know! She's always smiling and being funny.

b) Mary-Ann is a very ____pessimistic____ girl, she never believes things will be ok.

c) Chris's father is very ____hard-working____, he has two jobs.

d) My sister is a very ____tidy____ person, her room is always neat and clean.

e) Colin is always ____rude____ to his classmates. He is always bad to them.

6) Now, on your notebook, use the words from the previous exercise to write sentences about people you know.

Let's listen n' speak

1 **Listen to the continuation of Paul and Justin's conversation and answer the questions.**

a) Why didn't Paul invite Clara out?
_____

b) When was Clara sick?
_____

c) How does Paul feel when he is near Clara?
_____

d) Is Clara a popular person? Justify.
_____

e) Is Paul an outgoing person or a shy one?
_____

f) According to Justin, what are Paul's characteristics?
_____

g) What characteristics are they talking about?

- ( ) Physical characteristics.
- ( ) Personality traits.

h) Complete the chart with the characteristics you listen.

Paul	Clara

i) Who is the only character that is not described in the audio? _____

2 **Choose four friends to play with you. Tell them a sentence about one of your classmates, but do not say the name. Your partners have to guess who the person is.**

> **A:** This person sits near the teacher. This person has brown hair and green eyes. This person is very friendly and nice.
> **B:** I know! It's Leticia!

Let's practice

1 Read the following comic strip and analyze it.

a) When Garfield says "*used to post our selfies*", what does it mean?

- ◯ It means a past habit.
- ◯ It means a current habit.

GLOSSARY

Folks: pessoas, povo.

2 Label the following sentences as **T** (true) or **F** (false) according to your habits.

a) ◯ I used to wear glasses.

b) ◯ I used to swim.

c) ◯ I did not use to like vegetables.

d) ◯ I did not use to be funny.

e) ◯ I used to have a toy collection.

f) ◯ I did not use to go to bed early.

LANGUAGE PIECE

Used to

It is used to refer to things that were true over a period of time in the past. It refers to past habits and repeated past actions.

3 Look at Milton's appearance change and write sentences with **used to**. Follow the example.

> *He used to have crooked teeth.*

_____

_____

_____

_____

Vocabulary hint

Used to is pronounced with a short sound.

I **used to** /just tu/ have curly hair.

You **used to** /just tu/ be funny.

She **used to** /just tu/ have a tattoo.

He **used to** /just tu/ interact more.

They **used to** /just tu/ have a wart on the nose.

110

CHAPTER 3

Let's read n' write

1 Let's find out more about Gru's family. Read the files and answer the questions.

A FAMILY OF STRANGE, BUT TIGHT-KNIT CHARACTERS. MOST OF THEM ARE NOT BLOOD-RELATED, BUT EVEN SO, THEY ARE FAMILY ALL THE SAME.

BADASS FAMILY

FELONIUS GRU

The strong, smart, big, hot-tempered, yet reluctant and serious protagonist who has a Russian accent.

THE GIRLS

Margo – the oldest, cynical, somewhat bossy, yet the coolest of the three girls. She acts as a guardian to her younger sisters, and as such is slow to trust anyone.
Edith – middle, sarcastic, curious, and the hang loose of the three girls. Somewhat disagreeable, she likes to scare her siblings, but is easily irritated when Agnes sings.
Agnes – the youngest, tenderest, and the most joyful of the three girls. She is an oddball who loves unicorns and anything that's fluffy.

LUCY

Lucy Wilde is a cunning secret agent who has teamed up with Gru. She loves one-upping Gru with her quirky gadgets and has perfected her own form of martial arts.

DRU GRU

Dru is Gru's long-lost identical twin brother. Dru has a full head of blonde hair, wears all-white clothing, and presents a good-humored and sociable personality.

MARLENA GRU
Gru and Dru's mother and Robert's ex-wife is a very strong and skillful martial artist.

DR. NEFARIO

Gru's hearing-impaired gadget man and Mad Scientist friend, builder of the devices Gru uses in his schemes.

THE MINIONS

An army of small, yellow, cute, loyal, and childish goggled humanoids.

KYLE

Gru's unique pet.

GLOSSARY

Blood-related: consanguíneo.
Bossy: mandão, mandona, autoritário.
Childish: infantil.
Coolest: o mais legal.
Cunning: astuto, hábil.
Devices: dispositivos.
Disagreeable: desagradável.
Fluffy: fofo.
Gadgets: dispositivos.
Goggled: esbugalhado.
Hang loose: descolado, desencanado, largado.
Hearing-impaired: deficiente auditivo.
Hot-tempered: impetuoso, irritável.
Joyful: alegre.
Long-lost: perdido há muito tempo.
Loyal: leal, fiel.
Oddball: excêntrico.
One-upping (to one up): superar, ser melhor do que alguém.
Quirky: peculiar.
Tenderest: o mais sensível, delicado.
Tight-knit: unido.
Twin: gêmeo.

Based on: <www.animationsource.org/despicableme/en/info_chars/&id_film=199>. Access: July 2018.

a) Who is this person? Read the description and write the correct name.

- She is the bossy sister and acts as their guardian. She does not trust anyone. _____
- He is strong, smart, serious, big, and hot-tempered guy. _____
- She is the middle sister. She is curious and has a tomboy style. _____
- He is a scientist and a gadget man who creates lots of devices. _____
- She is a cunning person who has her own form of martial arts. _____
- She is the youngest sister. She is tender and joyful. _____
- He is a twin brother and has a good-humored and sociable personality. _____
- She is very good at martial arts. _____
- They are the loyal humanoids. _____
- An unusual and unique kind of pet. _____

b) What is its synonym? Match.

- childish
- hot-tempered
- joyful
- tender
- loyal
- cunning

- easily upset
- affectionate
- faithful
- happy
- immature
- imaginative

c) Now, working with a dictionary, match the opposites.

- childish
- hot-tempered
- joyful
- tender
- loyal
- cunning

- unimaginative
- upset
- unreliable
- easy-going
- unloving
- wise

d) What is a humanoid? _____

2 Thinking about the text, answer.

a) What kind of text is this? _____

b) What kind of information does this text present?

_____

_____

c) What is the aim of this text?

- ( ) To announce a movie.
- ( ) To sell a product.
- ( ) To describe a person.

d) What kind of text is used on the profile? Mark all that applies.

- ( ) Descriptive.
- ( ) Informative
- ( ) Narrative.
- ( ) Explanatory.
- ( ) Instructive.
- ( ) Persuasive.

3 Work with a friend. Choose four famous people or movie characters to make a profile description. Collect as much information as you can about each of them. Afterwards, organize your findings like the profile you read in the previous text.

CHAPTER 4

||| Citizenship moment |||

The Universal Declaration of HUMAN RIGHTS

It states basic rights and fundamental freedoms to which all human beings are entitled.

You have the responsibility to RESPECT THE RIGHTS OF OTHERS.

NO SLAVERY. Nobody has any right to make another person a slave.

Everyone has the right to life, FREEDOM, AND SAFETY.

NO TORTURE. Nobody has any right to hurt or to torture another person.

The Right to Seek a SAFE PLACE TO LIVE.

NOBODY SHOULD TRY TO HARM THE GOOD NAME OF OTHER PERSON, or come into a home, open letters, or bother a person or his/her family without a good reason.

We all have the right to GO TO WHEREVER WE WANT to in our own country and to travel as we wish.

NOBODY HAS THE RIGHT to imprison or deport another person without a good reason.

DON'T DISCRIMINATE. These rights belong to everybody, no matter the race, religion or nationality.

WE ALL HAVE THE RIGHT to belong to a country.

We are all born FREE AND EQUAL.

We're Always INNOCENT Till Proven Guilty.

We're All EQUAL Before the Law.

No one can take away any of YOUR RIGHTS.

If someone is put on trial, this should be in PUBLIC.

Your Human Rights are PROTECTED BY LAW.

GLOSSARY

Belong: pertencer.
Entitled, (to be entitled): ter direito a algo.
Freedoms: liberdades.
Guilty: culpado.
Harm: prejudicar.
Imprison: aprisionar.
Put on trial (to be put on trial): colocado em julgamento, julgado (ser colocado em julgamento, ser julgado).
Seek: procurar.
Slavery: escravidão.
Take away: levar embora; tomar.

Cristiane Viana

Based on: *What are human rights*, available at: <https://kidworldcitizen.org/human-rights-lessons-kids/>; *Human rights day*, available at: <www.huffpostbrasil.com/entry/human-rights-day_n_4420841>; *United Nations Universal Declaration of Human Rights*, available at: <www.youthforhumanrights.org/what-are-human-rights/universal-declaration-of-human-rights/introduction.htm>. Access: July 2018.

Let's practice

1 Say if the statement is T (true) or F (false).

a) ◯ We are all born free and equal.

b) ◯ The human rights do not belong to everybody. There are differences depending on the race, religion or nationality.

c) ◯ Everyone has the right to life, freedom and safety.

d) ◯ No slavery. Nobody has any right to make other person a slave.

e) ◯ There are a few people that can take away your rights.

f) ◯ We're not all equals before the law.

g) ◯ Your human rights are protected by law.

h) ◯ We're always guilty till proven innocent.

i) ◯ We have the right to seek a safe place to live.

j) ◯ You do not have to respect the rights of others.

2 Now, rewrite the false statements from the previous exercise, so that they are true.

_____
_____
_____
_____
_____
_____

3 In your opinion, what are the four most important rights listed on the infographic? List them on your notebook and tell the reasons why you chose them.

EXPLORING

- *Whoever you are*, by Mem Fox (author) and Leslie Staub (illustrator). HMH Books for Young Readers.

- *I'm Like You, You're Like Me: A Book About Understanding and Appreciating Each Other*, by Cindy Gainer (author) and Miki Sakamoto (illustrator). Free Spirit Publishing.

- *People*, by Peter Spier. Doubleday Books for Young Readers.

PROJECT

Human Rights

Have you ever heard about Human Rights? Form small groups and research about it: its history, its articles, who fiscalizes it etc. Once you gather all the information, prepare a summary with all the main information about it and discuss it with your classmates.

UNIT 8
WHAT IS THE WEATHER LIKE?

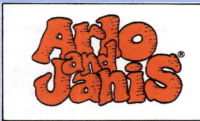

||| Get ready |||

1 Observe the pictures. What are they about?

_____

2 Read the following weather definitions and label them accordingly.

> image I – **1** • image II – **2** • image III – **3** • none – **N**

- ( ) hot
- ( ) warm
- ( ) cold
- ( ) cloudy
- ( ) rainy
- ( ) partially cloud
- ( ) clear
- ( ) sunny
- ( ) windy
- ( ) stormy

3 In the image III, what do you think the character means with the sentence "*Saturday looks like a good day for sweatpants*"?

_____

_____

_____

(III)

117

CHAPTER 1

Let's practice

1 Choose the best adjectives from the box to describe each picture.

> clear • cold • dry • freezing • humid • rainy • sunny • wet
> cloudy • cool • foggy • hot • icy • snowy • warm • windy

a)

_____

b)

_____

c)

_____

d)

_____

e)

_____

f)

_____

g)

_____

h)

_____

118

2 Complete the sentences with the best adjective from the box.

> cold • foggy • hot • snowy • warm
> dull • frosty • rainy • sunny • windy

a) Don't go outside. It is _____ and your cold can get worst.

b) It is _____ today. Take the umbrella.

c) Look at the trees moving! It is _____ today.

d) It's _____ today. Let's make a snowman.

e) It is _____ outside. I can hardly see anything.

f) The wind is _____. Put a scarf to protect yourself.

g) It is _____ today. Better be prepared to anything.

h) The weather is _____. Let's go for a walk.

i) I like the summer weather. It is _____ and _____ .

3 What is the weather like in each picture?

a)

c)

b)

d)

- ◯ foggy
- ◯ freezing

- ◯ rainy
- ◯ snowy

- ◯ winter
- ◯ windy

Let's listen n' speak

1 Listen to the Grover forecast and answer the questions.

a) Number the images according to the forecast you hear.

b) Match the weather, the piece of clothing and the temperature mentioned.

I. snowy   **II.** sunny   **III.** rainy

c) Say if it the sentences are **T** (true) or **F** (false).

- ◯ It is a sunny day, put on your coat.
- ◯ It is sunny, put on your sunglasses.
- ◯ It is snowy, you should get your coat.
- ◯ It is rainy, make sure you carry an umbrella.

2 What is the forecast for these cities? Talk about them with a partner.

a) MONTREAL

c) RIO BRANCO

b) BUDAPEST

d) CHAPECÓ

CHAPTER 2

Let's practice

1 Describe the weather in the images using the verbs from the box in the past continuous affirmative form.

> to blow • to drizzle • to rain • to shine • to snow • to thunder

a)
_____

d)
_____

b)
_____

e)
_____

c)
_____

f)
_____

2 Complete with the affirmative form of the past continuous.

a) Tom and Pam _____ scrambled eggs this morning. (to prepare)

b) The girls _____ the flowers to make a garland. (to cut)

c) The students _____ a lot for the test. (to study)

d) You and I _____ a movie yesterday. (to watch)

LANGUAGE PIECE

Past continuous – affirmative form

Subject pronoun + auxiliary verb in the past (to be) + main verb (+ -ing) + complement.

You were observing the wind.

She was enjoying the cold with some hot chocolate.

121

3. Rewrite the sentences using the negative form of the past continuous.

a) It was raining yesterday.
___

b) Carol and Mark were skiing last week.
___

c) It was snowing on Sunday.
___

d) My parents loved that it was thundering last night.
___

e) Edna was drinking water when she saw the news.
___

f) The children were enjoying their vegetables at lunch earlier today.
___

4. Choose the correct form of the verbs.

a) The children (was doing / were doing) their homework when I got home.

b) Carl (was watching / were watching) television when the telephone rang.

c) Where (was she working / were she worked) last July?

d) My head (was ached / was aching), that's why I went home.

e) Her English (was not improved / was not improving), that's why she took an immersion course.

f) What (were you doing / were you done) at the time of the incident?

5. Now, write five true sentences telling things you were not doing yesterday.

___
___
___
___

LANGUAGE PIECE

Past continuous – negative form

Subject pronoun + auxiliary verb in the past (to be) + not + main verb (+ -ing) + complement.

I was not playing in the snow.
You were not observing the wind.

122

6 Write questions for the following sentences.

a) _____

Yes, she was eating a salad for lunch.

b) _____

No, it was not raining last Saturday.

c) _____

Yes, Matt and Chris were sleeping in their bedroom.

d) _____

No, it was not thundering and drizzling last night.

e) _____

Yes, Julian and Marcel were playing video game instead of doing their homework.

f) _____

No, they were not traveling to Rio Branco. They were going to Manaus.

> **LANGUAGE PIECE**
>
> **Past continuous – interrogative form**
>
> Auxiliary verb in the past (to be) + subject pronoun + main verb (+ -ing) + complement?
>
> Were you observing the wind?
>
> Was she enjoying the cold weather with some hot chocolate?

7 Look at Finney's yesterday routine. Write questions about it.

> **Vocabulary hint**
> **The /-ng/ sound**
> It is a nasal sound.
> - observing
> - traveling
> - relaxing
> - organizing
> - sailing
>
> TRACK 23

_____
_____
_____
_____
_____
_____

Let's listen n' speak

1 Listen to Dalir talking to his grandma Emily and answer the questions.

a) What were Dalir and Emily talking about?

_____

b) Say if the sentence is **T** (true) or **F** (false).

- ( ) Emily and Dalir are not family.
- ( ) The wildfire is over by now.
- ( ) Emily cleaned a lot while she was at Sara's.
- ( ) People were moved during the wildfire.
- ( ) Dalir was at home during the game.
- ( ) About six hundred military personnel fought the fire across the province.

c) Complete the gaps to complete the summary of their dialogue.

> Dalir _____ his grandma because he was _____.
>
> She is fine and finally _____ home. _____
>
> the woods were burning, people were being evacuated. _____
>
> the wildfire, around _____ people were moved. The regions of
>
> Saskatchewan and _____ were in great danger.

d) Who said what? Write **E** for Emily and **D** for Dalir.

- ( ) It's over now, right?
- ( ) You just cannot stop making food.
- ( ) La Ronge became a ghost town during the evacuation.
- ( ) During the fire they were still getting people out.
- ( ) During this time about 600 military personnel were dispatched.
- ( ) I was playing ball while it was still warm.

Let's read n' write

1) Analyze the following weather forecast.

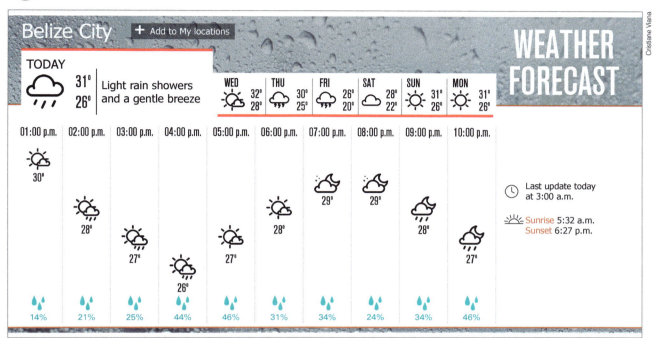

Você sabia que existem diferentes formas de medir a temperatura? Enquanto no Brasil utilizamos a escala **Celsius**, nos países de língua inglesa é usada a escala **Fahrenheit**.

0° C = 32 °F   100 °C = 212 °F

GLOSSARY

Sunrise: nascer do sol.
Sunset: pôr do sol.

a) Label the sentences as **T** (true) or **F** (false) according to the weather forecast.

- ◯ It was rainy on Saturday.
- ◯ It was rainy on Friday.
- ◯ There was a thunderstorm on Wednesday.
- ◯ It was rainy on Monday and Thursday.
- ◯ It was sunny on Monday.
- ◯ It was cloudy on Saturday.

b) When was it sunny?

c) What were the maximum and the minimum temperatures for Thursday?
___

d) When was it warmer during that day?
___

e) When did the humidity reach its highest point on that day?
___

f) When was the sunrise on that day?
___

g) What was the weather forecast for Belize that day?
___
___

2 What do these images mean?

a)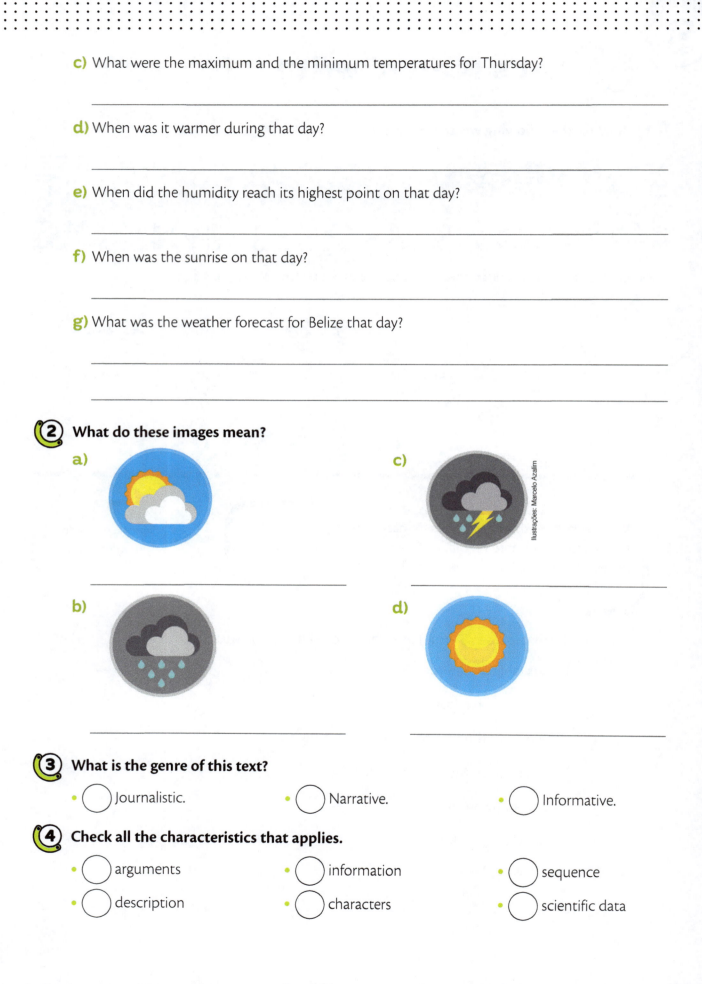

b)

c)

d)

3 What is the genre of this text?

- ( ) Journalistic.
- ( ) Narrative.
- ( ) Informative.

4 Check all the characteristics that applies.

- ( ) arguments
- ( ) information
- ( ) sequence
- ( ) description
- ( ) characters
- ( ) scientific data

5 Forecasting. How about creating your own forecast? Team up with two friends and choose a city (it can be your own) to create a weather forecast. Gather all the climate information available about it and follow the News forecast for the city during some days. Prepare your data to be presented to your classmates. You can make posters, handouts, use your imagination.

Look at the forecast example below:

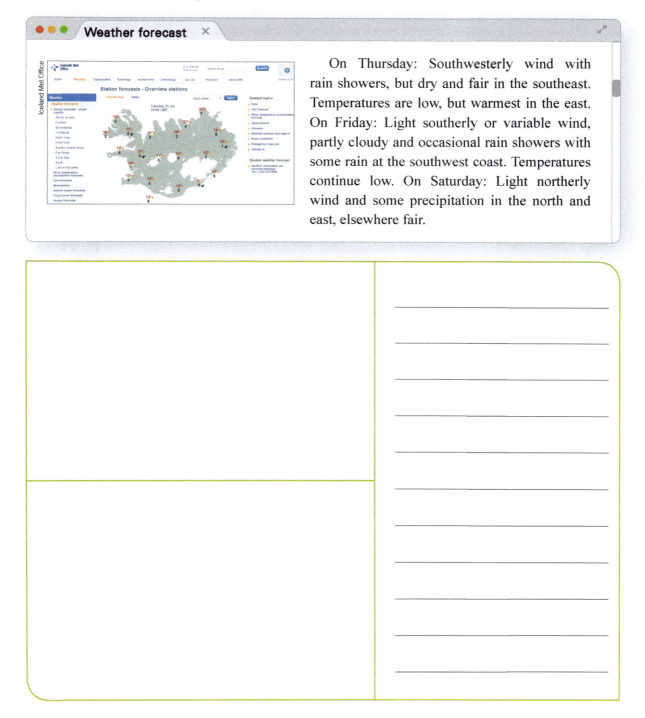

On Thursday: Southwesterly wind with rain showers, but dry and fair in the southeast. Temperatures are low, but warmest in the east. On Friday: Light southerly or variable wind, partly cloudy and occasional rain showers with some rain at the southwest coast. Temperatures continue low. On Saturday: Light northerly wind and some precipitation in the north and east, elsewhere fair.

CHAPTER 4

||| Tying in |||
WEATHER EXTREMES
GLOBAL IMPACTS AND IRREVERSIBLE CHANGES

AFFECT LIVES AROUND THE WORLD. DAMAGE TO CROPS AND COASTLINE CHANGES PUT WATER SECURITY AT RISK.

Cristiane Viana

Our planet is increasingly experiencing dramatic climate and weather extremes. Climate change will have severe consequences, such as more frequent extreme **heat**, less **reliable** water resources, **diseases** moving into new ranges, and sea level rises.

A WARMER WORLD
Evidence suggests that the world is already **locked into** about **1.5 °C WARMING** above pre-industrial times.

PROJECTED WARMING WITHOUT CONCERTED ACTION

2080	4 °C
2060	3 °C
2040	2 °C
2030	1,5 °C

GLACIAL MELT

Heat extremes and the melting of glaciers will have adverse effects on agriculture, water supplies, and biodiversity. As glaciers dissapear, reduced water flow will affect farms, forests, freshwater fisheries, energy, and biodiversity.

As temperatures rise, species will migrate and some will face extinction.

THE TIME FOR ACTION IS NOW!

DROUGHT

3 °C

| JAN | FEB | MAR | APR | MAY | JUN |
| JUL | AUG | SEP | OCT | NOV | DEC |

1.5 MONTHS PER YEAR WITHOUT DROUGHT

4 °C

| JAN | FEB | MAR | APR | MAY | JUN |
| JUL | AUG | SEP | OCT | NOV | DEC |

6 MONTHS PER YEAR WITH MODERATE DROUGHT

SEVERE STORMS

80%
INCREASE

WEATHER VERSUS CLIMATE

Weather is a specific event or condition that happens over a period of hours or days.

Climate refers to the average weather conditions in a place over many years (usually at least 30 years).

Available at: <www.epa.gov/climatestudents/basics/concepts.html>. Access: July 2018.

---

5 WAYS GOVERNMENTS CAN TAKE ACTION NOW

Put a robust price on carbon
Create incentives to invest in renewable energy and low-carbon **growth**.

Remove harmful fossil fuel subsidies
The money captured by the 20% richest **household** with the fossil fuel subsidies can be targeted to help the poor.

Build low-carbon, climate-resilient cities
Help reduce emissions, while careful planning and infrastructure can help population adapt.

Implement climate-smart agriculture
It can build resilience to the effects of climate change, increase productivity and reduce emissions.

Accelerate energy efficiency and renewable energy use
Increase investment and encourage innovation.

GLOSSARY

Diseases: doenças.
Drought: seca.
Growth: crescimento.
Harmful: prejudicial.
Heat: calor, aquecimento.
Household: domicílio.
Locked into: estar preso(a).
Reliable: confiável.

Based on: The World Bank. *Series: Turn Down the Heat*. Available at: <www.worldbank.org/en/topic/climatechange/publication/turn-down-the-heat>; United States Environmental Protection Agency. Available at: <www.epa.gov/climatestudents/basics/concepts.html>. Access: July 2018.

Let's practice

1. What are the consequences of the continuous increase of global temperatures?

2. What are the consequences for glacial melting?

3. What will happen to some species as temperature rises?

4. How long will droughts be with a 4 °C temperature rise?

5. What can be done?

6. What is the weather like in your country? Is there any region with an extreme climatic problem?

EXPLORING

Weather!, by Rebecca Rupp, Melissa Sweet (illustrator) and Dug Nap (illustrator). Storey Books.

The Reasons for Seasons, by Gail Gibbons (author and illustrator). Holiday House Inc.

EXPLORING

The Day after Tomorrow, 2004.

Tá chovendo hambúrguer, 2009.

EXPLORING

Weather for kids
www.sciencekids.co.nz/weather.html

PROJECT

Brazilian regional climates

Team up in five groups. Each group will research the climate and the weather of a Brazilian region. Go deep in the research and find out all about the region's climate characteristics. After gathering all the information, make a model using all kinds of materials that, in your opinion, represent the region's climate and weather. Use tags to explain the main characteristics in the model.

REVIEW

1 Who are they? Match the pictures and the descriptions.

a) This is Jack. He has short, light brown hair and blue eyes. He is tall and thin.

b) This is me. I am tall and thin and I have short, light brown hair.

c) This is my sister, Megan. She is short and has long brown hair and brown eyes.

d) This is Carol. She has long, black and curly hair. She is tall and slim.

e) This is Sebastian. He has short afro black hair. He is really tall.

2 Which adjective describes them better?

> generous • reliable • selfish • shy • talkative • touchy

a) My brother gets easily offended and upset. He is _____.

b) Susan's mother can be trusted to do things well. She is _____.

c) Our teacher is always willing to help freely. He is _____.

d) My cousin only thinks of her own advantage. She is _____.

e) Mariana is not comfortable talking in front of strange people. She is _____.

f) Gabriela and Marcos are always chatting around during the class. They are _____.

3) Unscramble the words and make sentences using the past continuous form of the verbs.

a) talking was Joanne on the the during phone class

_____

b) as the while My the car kids were washing playing husband was

_____

c) math I was when my home mom studying arrived

_____

d) friend singing best while I was was My playing guitar the

_____

4) Analyze the following weather forecasts carefully and fill in the gaps with the missing information.

> cloudy • drizzle • hot • Monday • rainy
> Saturday • stormy • Sunday • sunny

a) _____: It's going to be cold and _____ all day long. It may even _____. Take your coats and boots out of the closet!

b) _____: Don't forget your umbrella! It's going to be cold, _____, and _____ all day long.

c) _____: It's a perfect day for visiting the park! It's going to be _____ and _____! Wherever you decide to go, enjoy your weekend!

DO NOT FORGET!

VERB TO BE IN THE PAST + MAIN VERB-(ING)

Past continuous
Used to talk about actions that were in progress at a certain moment in the past.

AFFIRMATIVE: Subject + verb to be (past) + verb(-ing) + complement
Edward was studying English last evening.

INTERROGATIVE: Verb to be (past) + subject + verb(-ing) + complement?
Was Edward studying English last evening?

NEGATIVE: Subject + verb to be (past) + not + verb(-ing) + complement.
Edward was not/wasn't studying English last evening.

What do you look like?

I'm…
- tall or short…
- chubby / fat or slim / thin…

I have…
- black / dark / blue / green / brown eyes.
- red / blond / brown / black / dark / curly / straight hair.

What are you like?

NEGATIVE: clumsy, absent-minded, selfish, lazy, jealous, hesitant.

POSITIVE: reliable, generous, brave, cheerful, easy-going, neat, sensible.

USED TO

Habits/facts that were true in a certain moment in the past, but that are not true any longer.

AFFIRMATIVE: She used to be my friend when we were kids.

INTERROGATIVE: Did she use to be my friend when we were kids?

NEGATIVE: She didn't use to be my friend when we were kids.

WHAT'S THE WEATHER LIKE TODAY?

It's… hot – sunny – warm – clear – cool – partially cloudy
cloudy – drizzling – rainy – humid – wet – stormy
windy – cold – foggy – freezing – snowy.

OVERCOMING CHALLENGES

(FEI-SP)

Preencha os espaços em branco com a forma verbal correta:

> When she _____, I _____ to do my work.

a) has arrived – had tried

b) arrived – was trying

c) arrives – was trying

d) has arrived – has tried

e) arrived – try

(UEL-PR)

> In the summer of 1926, an English golf enthusiast named Samuel Ryder _____ (I) _____ a friendly game between some British professionals and the American players during that year's Open.

Assinale a letra correspondente à alternativa que preenche corretamente a lacuna (I) da frase apresentada.

a) was watching

b) watches

c) will watch

d) is watching

e) has watched

(UECE – 2011)

In terms of tense, the sentences "*Katherine Rowe's blue-haired avatar was flying across a grassy landscape*", "*Some students had already gathered online.*" and "*On a square coffee table sat a short stack of original issues of the magazine…*" are respectively in the

a) present continuous, present perfect, simple past.

b) past perfect continuous, past perfect, past perfect.

c) past continuous, past perfect, simple past.

d) past continuous, simple past, simple present.

WORKBOOK

||| Unit 1 |||

1) Unscramble the letters and find some clothing items.

a) sajne _____

b) pac _____

c) ti-rshT _____

d) katjec _____

e) hosse _____

f) elogvs _____

2) What are they wearing? Describe their clothes.

a)

Laura is wearing

_____

_____

b)

Tamy is wearing

_____

_____

c)

Fred is wearing

_____

_____

d)

Paula is wearing

_____

_____

e)

Lucas is wearing

_____

_____

f)

Mathew is wearing

_____

_____

3 **Find nine clothing items in the word search.**

T	S	K	S	H	I	R	T	T	I	D	T	T	V	I
H	O	P	W	H	P	R	O	C	A	R	Q	R	K	G
X	C	Z	M	W	O	P	O	Q	I	H	L	A	C	Q
H	K	V	M	U	U	S	C	R	V	Y	G	I	L	J
U	S	S	S	X	S	H	O	E	S	T	Z	N	A	E
J	M	E	R	R	L	S	A	Y	N	D	V	E	L	A
L	R	B	O	W	X	G	T	T	E	P	P	R	I	N
S	K	I	R	T	S	K	I	R	T	K	H	S	T	S
T	Y	P	V	O	D	J	S	O	N	T	U	I	F	Y
U	S	C	R	V	T	S	H	I	R	T	A	X	P	Y
C	A	P	E	S	K	H	U	M	Q	B	G	M	X	V

4 **Make questions using how much, and answer them using the prices given.**

a) that – blue skirt ($7.99)

_____

_____

b) those – high heels ($99.99)

_____

_____

c) this – pair of jeans ($119.90)

_____

_____

d) these – red shorts ($24.30)

_____

_____

5 **Complete the sentences using how much is or how much are.**

a) _____ this nice cap?

b) _____ these shoes?

c) _____ the T-shirts?

d) _____ the blouse?

e) _____ those trainers?

f) _____ this coat?

g) _____ the trousers?

h) _____ the socks?

WORKBOOK

||| Unit 2 |||

1. Carol is preparing a picnic for herself and her friends. Look at the things that are on the table and check the sentences that are true.

a) ◯ There are some sandwiches.   d) ◯ There's some juice.

b) ◯ There's a chocolate cake.   e) ◯ There are some pancakes.

c) ◯ There's some soda.   f) ◯ There aren't any mangoes.

2. Now, answer the following questions about the picnic table from the previous exercise.

a) Are there any mangoes?   c) Is there an apple?

_____   _____

b) Is there any juice?   d) Are there any sandwiches?

_____   _____

3. Mark if the items are **C** (countable) or **U** (uncountable).

a) ◯ apple   f) ◯ jam   k) ◯ steak
b) ◯ bread   g) ◯ juice   l) ◯ sugar
c) ◯ butter   h) ◯ pear   m) ◯ carrots
d) ◯ egg   i) ◯ pepper   n) ◯ water
e) ◯ bags   j) ◯ rice

136

4 Choose the right quantifier to complete the sentences.

a) There aren't _____ chips to serve the guests. (any / some)

b) There is _____ salad on the table. (any / some)

c) She isn't going to bake _____ cookies today. (much / many)

d) There is _____ burger in the buffet. (a / any)

e) They didn't have _____ beef stew. (much / many)

f) Mary bought _____ cherries yesterday. (a little / a few)

g) There is _____ juice in the jar. (a little / a few)

h) Carla brought _____ bananas from the grocery store. (little / few)

i) There is _____ milk to bake the cake. (little / few)

5 Rewrite the sentences correcting the mistake in each one.

a) There is a few ice cream.

_____

b) There isn't some butter.

_____

c) Do we have many coffee?

_____

d) There isn't some cheese.

_____

e) I think I ate too many cake.

_____

6 Organize the quantifiers into the correct column.

a • a little • a lot of • any • much
a few • a lot • an • many • some

countable	uncountable

WORKBOOK

||| Unit 3 |||

1 Look at Sarah's list of abilities. Write sentences about it, using can or can't.

- cook delicious food ☑
- dance ballet ☒
- drive cars and trucks ☑
- ride a bike ☒
- sew ☒
- swim very well ☑

_____
_____
_____
_____
_____
_____

2 Fill in the gaps with the missing words. Then, complete the crossword puzzle with them.

1. Does your teacher _____ glasses?

2. Kids, you have to study _____ . Look at these bad grades!

3. Eating _____ is not good for children.

4. You can't use the _____ phone inside the classroom.

5. Do you and your classmates _____ rubbish?

6. Johnny, please, _____ your room.

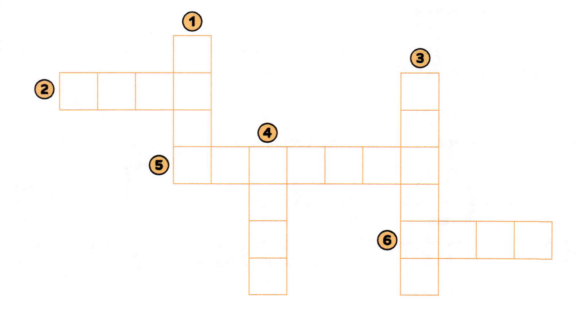

3 **Change the sentences into their negative form. Use contractions.**

a) Michael can sew well.

_____

b) Charlotte should study more.

_____

c) The kids can go to that party with you.

_____

d) I should visit my aunt at the hospital.

_____

4 **Number the sentences according to the label.**

> 1 – Knowledge of how or ability to do something.
> 2 – Permission to or possibility of doing something.
> 3 – Suggestion: it is or it is not a good thing to do.

a) ( ) They can watch TV late on weekends.

b) ( ) Allison, you should talk to your mom about this problem.

c) ( ) You can go home after this test.

d) ( ) My family and I can ski really well.

e) ( ) You should recycle all this rubbish.

f) ( ) We can play the piano, but not very well.

5 **Circle the best option.**

a) Can cook and bake different food and dishes really well:
- ( ) a chef.
- ( ) an athlete.
- ( ) an artist.

b) Can run and swim really well and fast:
- ( ) an athlete.
- ( ) an actor.
- ( ) an artist.

c) Can paint and draw really well:
- ( ) an actor.
- ( ) a chef.
- ( ) an artist.

WORKBOOK

Unit 4

1) What place in a city is this?

a) A place where you go to send letters. _____

b) A place where you can eat. _____

c) A building where people go to pray. _____

d) A place where people can borrow books. _____

e) An office where police officers work. _____

f) A building where people can see old things. _____

g) A place where doctors and nurses work. _____

h) A big shop where you can buy food and other things. _____

i) A place where you go to watch a film. _____

j) A place where people can buy medicines. _____

k) A place where children go to learn. _____

l) A place where people keep their money safe. _____

2) Choose the best option.

a) This is a very (polluted / clean) river. People can't drink its water.

b) I don't like this city. There is nothing to do and I'm usually (bored / exciting) here.

c) I love this street because it is so calm and (noisy / quiet)! I can even hear the birds singing.

d) Look at all these buildings: this is a very (old / modern) city. It is not old.

3) Match the columns.

a) Where do you live?

b) Do you like living here?

c) What places are there here?

d) What don't you like about here?

e) Where would you like to live?

- ( ) Yes, I really do!
- ( ) I don't like the traffic and the noise.
- ( ) There are beautiful waterfalls and parks.
- ( ) I would like to live in the countryside.
- ( ) I live in a modern city.

4 Look at the map and complete the sentences about it with the correct prepositions of place.

a) The school is _____ to the park.

b) The fire station is _____ the restaurant 'Food'.

c) The church is _____ the cafeteria.

d) The city square is _____ the church and the school.

e) There is a dog _____ the cafeteria.

5 Write the directions to get from the house to…

a) … the gas station. _____

_____

b) … the supermarket. _____

_____

_____

c) … the restaurant. _____

_____

WORKBOOK

||| Unit 5 |||

1. Write the sentences in the affirmative and negative form of the simple past.

a) I beg her not to make me sign up.

_____

_____

b) I need to sing a solo in front of the whole school.

_____

_____

c) I start going to play practices.

_____

_____

d) It messes up with my weight-lifting schedule.

_____

_____

2. Organize the words into the correct category.

adventure • detective • historical • news • poetry
biography • fantasy • horror • play • thriller

Kinds of text	Kinds of stories

3 Write the simple past form of the following verbs.

a) to add _____   d) to have _____

b) to cry _____   e) to come _____

c) to watch _____   f) to start _____

4 Write questions for the answers.

a) _____   c) _____
No, she didn't walk home from school.   The boys traveled to Australia.

b) _____   d) _____
The show started at 11 pm.   Yes, I washed my hair today.

5 Find and circle the mistakes and correct them in the line next to the sentence.

a) I relax at the beach last summer.

_____

b) Do you liked the movie last night?

_____

c) Yes, I did use my computer this morning.

_____

6 Complete the gaps with **was** or **were**. Then, rewrite the sentences in their negative form.

a) The students _____ inside the classroom when the class started this morning.

_____

b) Albert _____ at home last night.

_____

c) I _____ worried about the tests.

_____

d) My family and I _____ here last weekend.

_____

143

WORKBOOK

||| Unit 6 |||

1) Movies are connected with music through the soundtracks, among other aspects. Read the sentences below and mark T (true) or F (false) for the following statements.

a) ( ) A thriller movie has only romantic songs.

b) ( ) Violins are always played in adventure movies' soundtracks.

c) ( ) In a musical movie, each character usually knows how to dance and sing.

d) ( ) Comedies have a funny plot and charismatic actors.

e) ( ) The Oscar is a music prize for the best musicians in the world.

f) ( ) Many singers are also actors, like Demi Lovato, Jon Bon Jovi, and Miley Cirus.

2) Match the nouns according to their respective genre of movie.

a) alien

b) laugh

c) explore

d) kiss

e) monster

f) wizard

g) cowboy

h) explosion

- ( ) horror
- ( ) fantasy
- ( ) romance
- ( ) adventure
- ( ) action
- ( ) science fiction
- ( ) comedy
- ( ) western

3) Write the simple past form of the verbs and tell if they are R (regular) or I (irregular).

a) ( ) to take _____

b) ( ) to dream _____

c) ( ) to see _____

d) ( ) to learn _____

e) ( ) to read _____

f) ( ) to eat _____

g) ( ) to forget _____

h) ( ) to visit _____

i) ( ) to be _____

j) ( ) to use _____

4 Complete the sentences with the simple past form of the following verbs.

go • get up • have • meet • run • swim

a) Yesterday, I _____ early, at about seven o´clock.

b) I _____ some fruits for breakfast.

c) Then, I _____ to the sports center.

d) I _____ 500 meters in the swimming pool and then

e) I _____ 5 kilometers.

f) At lunchtime, I _____ my friends in a coffee shop.

5 Rewrite the following sentences in the simple past tense.

a) I **think** they **are** in Mexico, not Spain.

_____

b) **Do** your sisters **help** each other with their homework?

_____

c) The flight attendant **doesn't put** enough sugar in my coffee.

_____

d) My brother **is** a pilot. He **flies** to many countries.

_____

6 What is this musical instrument?

a)
_____

b)
_____

c)
_____

d)
_____

WORKBOOK

||| Unit 7 |||

1) What do they look like?

a)

_____

_____

c)

_____

_____

b)

_____

_____

d)

_____

_____

2) Look at the chart and make sentences using the checked characteristics.

	Green eyes	Brown eyes	Blond hair	Gray hair
Priscila		x		x
Courtney	x		x	
Hugo		x	x	
Yuri and Wanda	x			x

_____   _____

_____   _____

3) What is the opposite of...

a) ... honest? _____

b) ... reliable? _____

c) ... patient? _____

d) ... sensitive? _____

e) ... polite? _____

f) ... kind? _____

g) ... happy? _____

h) ... loyal? _____

4) Complete the sentences with the correct form of **used to** and the opposite of the underlined adjectives.

a) My neighborhood _____ be very sad, but after the construction of the new park, it became _____.

b) Did you _____ be chubby or _____ when you were a kid?

c) I didn't _____ be pessimistic when I was at college; I was usually very _____.

d) Bob _____ be so lazy, but look at him now: he's really _____!

e) When my children were younger, their room didn't _____ be tidy, it was always really _____.

5) Make sentences using **used to** and the complements given.

a) My mother – touchy – teenager
_____

b) I – tall – a child
_____

c) My siblings and I – funny – younger
_____

d) My teachers – happy – at school
_____

WORKBOOK

||| Unit 8 |||

1) Match the icons and the words, as in the example.

- ( ) rainy
- ( ) snowy
- ( ) sunny and hot
- ( ) windy
- ( ) stormy
- ( ) cloudy
- ( ) partially cloudy
- ( ) thundering
- ( ) drizzling

2) How was the weather yesterday around the world? Unscramble the words and complete the sentences correctly.

a) In Brazil (shining – was – sun – the)

_____

b) In Germany (was – the – blowing – wind)

_____

c) In England (thundering – was – it – and – raining)

_____

d) In India (and – it – drizzling – was – cold)

_____

3) Rewrite the following sentences in their affirmative, negative or interrogative forms as asked.

a) My friends and I were watching a film last night.

Negative: _____

Interrogative: _____

b) Were Jack and Bob studying math with you last week?

Affirmative: _____

Negative: _____

4 Look at the pictures and write negative sentences about what Julian wasn't doing yesterday afternoon.

a) to paint _____

b) to play the guitar _____

c) to play tennis _____

d) to ride a bike _____

e) to run _____

f) to play soccer _____

g) to fly a kite _____

5 Mark with an **X** the best option to complete each of the following sentences.

a) It _____ sunny yesterday… It was foggy and very cold.
- ( ) was
- ( ) were not
- ( ) was not

b) Ralph was _____ when his parents arrived home last evening.
- ( ) play
- ( ) to play
- ( ) playing

c) There were lots of clouds in the sky yesterday… I couldn't even see the sun. It was a _____ day.
- ( ) cloudy
- ( ) cloud
- ( ) foggy

d) You should wear boots and take your umbrella with you. It is _____.
- ( ) dry
- ( ) drizzling
- ( ) windy

e) You _____ sleeping when the storm began.
- ( ) were
- ( ) was
- ( ) are

149

EXPERT'S POINT I

It can be hard **to say no** to invitations. We usually don't want people to think we're **selfish**. More than that, we don't want to *be* selfish. But we, human beings, will often choose what is most satisfying in the present, rather than what will make us happier in the future – and **pleasing others** (and thinking of ourselves as generous) by saying "yes" to invitations we don't really want to accept tends to be far more pleasant in the present than saying "no." However, saying "yes" when we want to say "no" tends to **bite us later**, in the form of resentment and exhaustion.

■ HUMAN BEHAVIOUR

THREE STEPS TO SAY "NO" GRACEFULLY

Saying yes when we want to say no tends to bite us later.

By Christine L. Carter, PhD., Therapist.

[…]
We can make better decisions by picturing ourselves moments before the event in question. Would we be relieved if it were canceled? If so, we've gotta say no *now*, so that we don't find ourselves trying to **weasel out of** it later. Here's how:

1. Rehearse saying "no".

When we are stressed and tired, we tend to act habitually. Knowing this, we can train our brain to habitually say *no* rather than *yes* to requests by **rehearsing** a **go-to response** […].

Something simple – like, "That doesn't work for me this time" – is almost always sufficient.. […] Pick a **default** way to respond when you don't want to do something, and **practice saying it** before you need it.

2. Be clear about your priorities and truthful in your refusal.

Saying no is easier when we're clear about our **priorities**; it's even harder to decline a request when our reasons for doing so **seem** unimportant. […]

Be honest, but don't be afraid to be vague. Telling the truth is not the same as sharing more details than are necessary, even if someone asks why you can't help them out or come to their party. Detailed explanations imply that the other person can't **handle** a simple no – and they often lead to people solving your conflicts for you, when you don't really want them to.

If your "no" isn't accepted with grace, persist. Repeat your point calmly, *using the same words*. […]

If they still won't **back down**, tell them the truth about **how you are feeling**. For example: "I feel uncomfortable and a little angry when you continue to ask me even though I've declined." […]

3. Make your final decision.

Harvard psychologist Dan Gilbert has famously shown that when we can **change our mind**, we tend to be a lot less happy with our decisions. So, once we decline an invitation, we need to make an effort to focus on **the good that will come from saying no**, not the **regret** or **guilt** we might feel. Perhaps we will be better rested because we didn't go to a party, or we'll feel less resentful because we let someone else help out. Maybe saying no to one thing frees up time for another (more joyful) activity.

[…]

If you are feeling nervous about saying no, take a moment to call up the **respect for yourself** that you'd like others to feel for you. It takes courage to consider your own needs and priorities along with the needs of others. But it's worth it. **In the long run, the ability to say no is a little-known key to happiness.**

> **GLOSSARY**
>
> **Back down**: abandonar, desistir.
> **Change our mind (to change someone's mind)**: mudar de opinião.
> **Default**: padrão.
> **Go-to**: rápida, ágil.
> **Guilt**: culpa.
> **Handle**: lidar com.
> **Long run**: longo prazo.
> **Pleasing (to please)**: agradar.
> **Regret**: arrepender-se.
> **Rehearsing (to rehearse)**: ensaiando (ensaiar).
> **Seem**: parecer.
> **Selfish**: egoísta.
> **Weasel out of**: escapar ou evitar algo.

PROJECT

Practicing: how to say "No" gracefully

Are you ready to say "no" to an invitation? Think of polite ways of saying "no", write them down and choose the ones that best suit you. Then, in groups, practice it: you and your classmates should invite each other to boring activities and use what you have prepared in order to say "no" politely. The more you practice it, the easier it will be for you to say "no" gracefully in real life. Follow your teacher's instructions.

Expert's profile

Christine L. Carter

Christine L. Carter is a PhD sociologist and Senior Fellow at UC Berkeley's Greater Good Science Center, where she draws on scientific research to help people lead their most courageous, joyful, meaningful, and authentic lives. Dr. Carter also writes an award-winning blog, Brave Over Perfect, and is a contributor to US News & World Report online. Her work has earned her two nominations from the American Sociological Association for public sociology and an award from the Council on Contemporary Families.

Available at: <www.psychologytoday.com/us/blog/brave-over-perfect/201710/three-steps-say-no-gracefully>. Access: Aug. 2018.

EXPERT'S POINT II

Your **personality** influences everything: from the friends you choose to the **candidates** you vote for in a political election. Understanding your personality can give you **insight** into your **strengths and weaknesses**. It can also help you **gain** insight into how others see you.

■ TECNOLOGY

Psychologists Say There Are Only 5 Kinds of People in the World. Which One Are You?

Once you understand your personality type, it's easy to identify other people's too

By Amy Morin, Psychotherapist.

[...]

Most modern-day psychologists agree there are **five major personality types**. Referred to as the "five factor model", everyone possesses some degree of each.

1. Conscientiousness

People who rank highest in conscientiousness are **efficient, well-organized, dependable, and self-sufficient**. They prefer to plan things in advance and aim for high achievement. [...]

2. Extroversion

People who rank high in extroversion gain energy from social activity. They're **talkative** and **outgoing** and they're comfortable in the **spotlight**. Others may view them as **domineering** and attention-seeking. [...]

3. Agreeableness

Those who rank high in agreeableness are **trustworthy**, **kind**, and **affectionate** toward others. They're known for their pro-social behavior and they're often committed to volunteer work and altruistic activities. Other people may view them as naïve and overly passive. [...]

4. Openness to Experience

People who **rate** high in openness are known for their **broad** range of interests and vivid imaginations. They're curious and creative and they usually prefer variety over rigid routines. [...] Others may view them as **unpredictable** and **unfocused**. [...]

> **GLOSSARY**
>
> **Agreeableness**: agradabilidade.
> **Broad**: amplo.
> **Conscientiousness**: conscienciosidade.
> **Domineering**: dominador.
> **Extroversion**: extroversão.
> **Gain (to gain)**: ganhar.
> **Insight**: discernimento.
> **Neuroticism**: neuroticismo.
> **Openness**: abertura.
> **Rate (to rate)**: classificar, avaliar.
> **Spotlight**: holofote, local de destaque.
> **Unpredictable**: imprevisível.

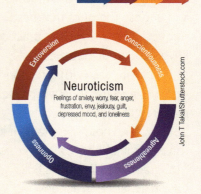

Psychological Personality Traits

5. Neuroticism

Neurotic people experience a high degree of emotional instability. They're more likely to be **reactive** and **excitable** and they report higher degrees of unpleasant emotions like anxiety and irritability. Other people may view them as **unstable** and **insecure**. […]

Understanding the basics of personality

Personality remains relatively stable over time. The personality traits you exhibited at age 7 are likely to predict much of your behavior as an adult.

Of course, you can **change** some of your personality traits. It takes hard work and effort to make big changes, but most scientists agree that it is possible.

PROJECT

Which personality model fits me?

Do you know what kind of person you are based on the five-factor model theory? Think of your most relevant personality traits and write them down. Then, read the article again and try to find which personality model best fits you. When you are done, work in small groups and compare your ideas with your classmates'. Do people see you the same way? Do you see people the same way they see themselves? Why? Follow your teacher's instructions and discuss these points.

Expert's profile

Amy Morin, LCSW

Amy Morin

Amy Morin is a psychotherapist whose mission is to make the world a stronger place. Her education and expertise as a psychotherapist, combined with her personal experiences, give her a unique perspective on mental strength. She presented the concept of mental strength in her article, *13 Things Mentally Strong People Don't Do*, read by more than 50 million people. Her advice has been featured by numerous media outlets, and she gives lectures across the globe to provide trainings, workshops, and keynote speeches that teach people how to build their mental muscle.

Available at: <www.inc.com/amy-morin/psychologists-say-there-are-5-personality-types-heres-how-to-tell-which-one-you-.html>. Access: Aug. 2018.

FOCUS ON CULTURE I
HOW DO BRAZILIANS SPEND THEIR MONEY?
FROM HOUSING TO LEISURE

THE AVERAGE HOUSEHOLD INCOME PER CAPITA IN BRAZIL WAS R$ 1,268.31 IN 2017

FOOD
16.1%
Restaurants and food markets

HEALTH
5.9%
Drugstores, hospitals, and health insurance

HOUSING
29.2%
Rent, mortgage, and other expenses and services

CLOTHING
4.5%
Clothes, shoes, and accessories

PHYSIOLOGICAL NEEDS – 55.7%

Based on: IBGE, Diretoria de Pesquisa, Coordenação de Trabalho e Rendimento, Pesquisa de Orçamentos Familiares 2008-2009. Available at: <ftp://ftp.ibge.gov.br/Orcamentos_Familiares/Pesquisa_de_Orcamentos_Familiares_2008_2009/Perfil_das_Despesas_no_Brasil/POF2008_2009_perfil.pdf>; IBGE, Diretoria de Pesquisa, Coordenação de Trabalho e Rendimento. Pesquisa Nacional por Amostra de Domicílios Contínua – PNAD Contínua – 2017. Available at: <ftp://ftp.ibge.gov.br/Trabalho_e_Rendimento/Pesquisa_Nacional_por_Amostra_de_Domicilios_continua/Renda_domiciliar_per_capita/Renda_domiciliar_per_capita_2017.pdf>. Access: July 2018.

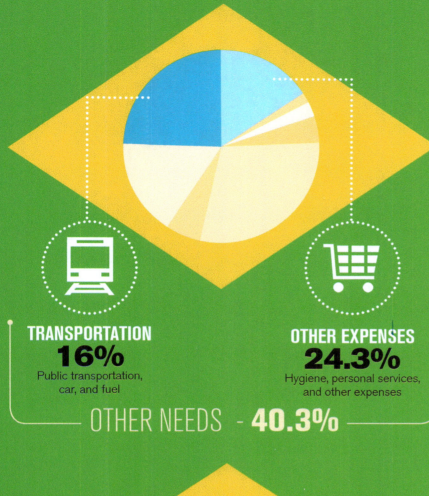

TRANSPORTATION
16%
Public transportation, car, and fuel

OTHER EXPENSES
24.3%
Hygiene, personal services, and other expenses

OTHER NEEDS - **40.3%**

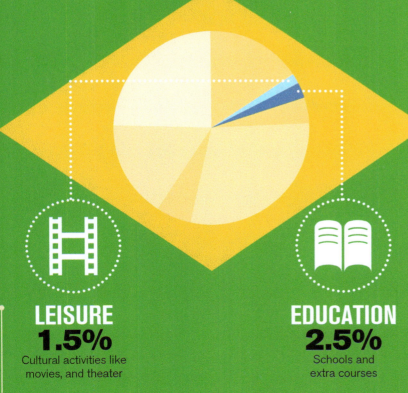

LEISURE
1.5%
Cultural activities like movies, and theater

EDUCATION
2.5%
Schools and extra courses

SELF-ACTUALIZATION NEEDS - **4%**

PROJECT

Discussion and pie chart

In small groups, calculate the value in *reais* of the percentages shown in the infographic. You may use the average household income per capita and the proportion rules. Your teacher will help you with these calculations.

Then, answer the following questions with your group.

- Do you think Brazilians spend their money wisely? Why?
- How much, in your opinion, should Brazilians spend on housing? And on leisure? Why?
- Do you think the distribution shown in the infographic is adequate? Why?
- Can you think of a better money distribution for Brazilians to spend their money monthly?
- Would that reality be possible considering the Brazilian society? Why?

Plan a balanced distribution of money, according to what your group believes to be ideal. Then, using the average household income per capita in Brazil, draw a pie chart that represents the distribution of money your group has designed. Finally, present it to your classmates justifying your ideas.

FOCUS ON CULTURE 11

HOW'S THE WEATHER?

WEATHER, CLIMATE AND EVEN SEASONS CAN BE COMPLETELY DIFFERENT DEPENDING ON THE HEMISPHERE YOU ARE IN.

EARTH'S SEASONS

The seasons in the Southern Hemisphere are the opposite of those in the Northern Hemisphere. When the Northern Hemisphere is facing the sun – receiving the most direct sunlight and, therefore, experiencing summertime –, the Southern Hemisphere is tilted away from it, experiencing less direct sunlight and the winter season.

*(not to scale)

DID YOU KNOW THAT...?

The North Pole and the South Pole receive **full sunlight 24 HOURS PER DAY** throughout the entire **summer**, and **full darkness 24 HOURS PER DAY** throughout the entire **winter**.

156

WEATHER AND SEASONS AROUND THE WORLD

The highest temperature ever registered was
56.7 °C
in California, U.S.A., in 1913.

NORTHERN HEMISPHERE

SUMMER

June 21st to September 21st

FALL

September 22nd to December 20th

WINTER

December 21st to March 19th

SPRING

March 20th to June 20th

SOUTHERN HEMISPHERE

SUMMER

December 21st to March 19th

FALL

March 20th to June 20th

WINTER

June 21st to September 22nd

SPRING

September 23rd to December 20th

The lowest temperature ever registered, outside Antarctica, was
−68 °C
in Oymyakon, Russia, in 1933.

PROJECT

Answer the following questions with your classmates.

- How are the hemispheres divided? In which hemisphere do you live?
- How are the seasons defined?
- Why are the seasons in the Southern Hemisphere opposite to the ones in the Northern Hemisphere?
- How are the seasons of the year where you live?

In small groups, choose a major city from each hemisphere quadrant, including your own city, and research the seasons and the weather conditions related to them. Use the following questions as a guideline to do your research:

- When does each season start and finish?
- What are each season's characteristics?
- How do local people survive to extreme?
- Are there any special characteristics related to this city's weather, like flooding or other phenomena like El Niño or La Niña?
- Are there any Global Warming effects over the temperatures and weather in these cities?

Use a globe or a world map to search for the cities, a Geographic Student World Atlas and your teacher's suggested websites to take notes, and design a poster with all the information you found out. Present it to your classmates.

Based on: *Highest recorded temperature*. Guinness World Records. Available at: <www.guinnessworldrecords.com/world-records/highest-recorded-temperature>; *When do the four seasons officially begin?* (FAQ - Time). National Physical Laboratory. Available at: <www.npl.co.uk/science-technology/time-frequency/time/faqs/when-do-the-four-seasons-officially-begin-(faq-time)>; *Why Are the Seasons Reversed in the Southern Hemisphere?* Reference. Available at: <www.reference.com/science/seasons-reversed-southern-hemisphere-295a6285003aa574>; *Lowest temperature – inhabited*. Guinness World Records. Available at: <www.guinnessworldrecords.com/world-records/lowest-temperature-inhabited>. Access: July 2018.

LANGUAGE COURT

||| Unit 1 |||

Page 8

Here is a set of words related to clothing.

Clothing items (general)		Clothing items (sportswear)	Accessories	
Belt	Pullover	Bikini	Bag	Necklace
Blazer	Raincoat	Helmet	Cap	Ring
Blouse	Socks	Jogging suit	Earrings	Scarf
Cardigan	Shirt	Ski wear	Glasses	Sunglasses
Coat	Shorts	Sweatshirt	Gloves	Tie
Dress	Skirt	Swimsuit	Hairband	Wool hat
Jacket	Suit	Tracksuit	Hat	Wristwatch
Jeans	T-shirt	Trainers	Jewelry	
Jumper	Trousers	Uniform	**Footwear items**	
Overcoat	Underclothes	Wetsuit	Boots	Shoes
Pajamas	Vest		High heels	Slippers / flip-flops
			Sandals	Sneakers

Page 11

The **demonstrative pronouns** are used to point to something specific within a sentence. They can indicate items near or far in space or time that can be either singular or plural. Look:

	Near	Far
Singular	This	That
Plural	These	Those

Look at some examples:
This is my mother's ring. → The ring is a **singular** item and it is **near** the speaker.
That looks like my father's car. → The car is a **singular** item and it is **far** from the speaker.
These are my keys. → The keys are **plural** items and they are **near** the speaker.
Those are their bags. → The bags are **plural** items and they are **far from** the speaker.

Page 12

The interrogative form **how much** is used to ask questions about the price of something. It can be used with both singular and plural nouns. Look at the examples:

Singular	Plural
How much is that painting? *It is $ 80.*	How much are those shoes? *They are $ 120.*
How much is that ring? *It is $ 13.*	How much are the pajamas? *They are $ 32.*

||| Unit 2 |||

Page 22

Here is a set of words related to food.

Fruits	Vegetables	Meat	Grains	Diary	Other Foods
Apple	Asparagus	Bacon	Bread	Butter	Honey
Apricot	Beans	Beef	Cereal	Cheese	Jelly
Avocado	Beet	Chicken	Cookie	Milk	Oil
Banana	Cabbage	Cod	Flour	Yogurt	Pepper
Berry	Carrot	Fish	Pasta / spaghetti		Salad dressing
Cantaloupe	Cauliflower	Ham	Pie	**Candies**	Salt
Cherry	Celery	Hamburger	Rice	Cake	Sauce
Coconut	Corn	Hot dog	Toast	Candy	Vinegar
Grape	Cucumber	Lamb	Wheat	Chocolate	
Lemon	Garlic	Meat loaf		Ice cream	**Dishware**
Orange	Green beans	Pork			Bowl
Peach	Lettuce	Poultry	**Drinks**	**Meals**	Cup
Pear	Onion	Rabbit	Coffee	Breakfast	Fork
Pineapple	Pea	Roast	Juice	Dinner	Glass
Plum	Potato	Salmon	Milk	Lunch	Knife
Strawberry	Pumpkin	Sausage	Soda	Snack	Napkin
Tomato	Sweet potato	Seafood	Tea	Supper	Plate
Watermelon		Turkey	Water		Spoon

Page 25

Nouns can be either **countable** or **uncountable**. The **countable** nouns are the ones that can be counted into units; it means each item can be enumerated and has singular and plural forms. They can be used with articles such as **a**, **an**, **the**, numbers or some **quantifiers**. For example:
- I want **an** apple, **a** pear, **two** bananas and **the** bowl to prepare the fruit salad.

The **uncountable** nouns are also called **mass** nouns and are the ones that come in a state that cannot be counted or enumerated by units. It means that they regularly do not have a plural form and that is why they are commonly considered singular nouns. They can stand alone or be used with some quantifiers. For example:
- I need **some** flour, butter and milk to bake the cake.

Page 26

To talk about quantities and amounts we use the **quantifiers**. The quantifiers can be used with only **countable**, only **uncountable** or both types of nouns. Look at the table:

Countable		Uncountable	
A couple of	Hundreds of	A little	Least
A few	Many	A bit of	Little
Both	Several	A great deal of	Much
Each	Thousands of	A good deal of	Not much
Either		A cup of	
Fewer		Less	

Both	
All	Plenty of
Any	Tons of
A lot of	Some
A load of	Some
Enough	Some
Less	Some
Lots of	Some
More	Some
Most	Some
None of	Some

||| Unit 3 |||

Page 43

The modal verb **can** is one of the most used in English. It can express:
- Ability, skill:
I **can** speak Spanish.
My daughter **can** play the piano very well.

- Possibility, potential:
I **can** help her now.

- Permission:
You **can** drive my car.

- Request (interrogative sentences only):
Can you lend me your eraser?

As a modal verb, its form remains the same with all the personal pronouns and it is followed by verbs in the infinitive form without to. Take a look:
Sheila **can** **play** video game after doing her homework.
We **can** **ride** horses.

To form the negative, add **not** after the modal. Look:
Sheila **can**not (**can't**) **play** video game after doing her homework.
We **can**not (**can't**) **ride** horses.

Page 45

The modal verb **should** is used to express:
- Recommendation and advice:
Kevin **should** do his homework every day.

- To indicate something which is likely:
She **should** be here by noon.
(She left home at 9 and it takes her three hours to get here).

As a modal verb, its form remains the same with all the personal pronouns and it is followed by verbs in the infinitive form without to. Take a look:
Lia **should** **help** her parents with the household chores.
We **should** **go back** home now.

To form the negative, add **not** after the modal. Look:
Lia **should** **not** (**shouldn't**) **help** her parents with the household chores.
We **should** **not** (**shouldn't**) **go back** home now.

||| Unit 4 |||

Page 57

The **prepositions of place** are used to indicate where something is placed or the position of a thing or person. Take a look at them:

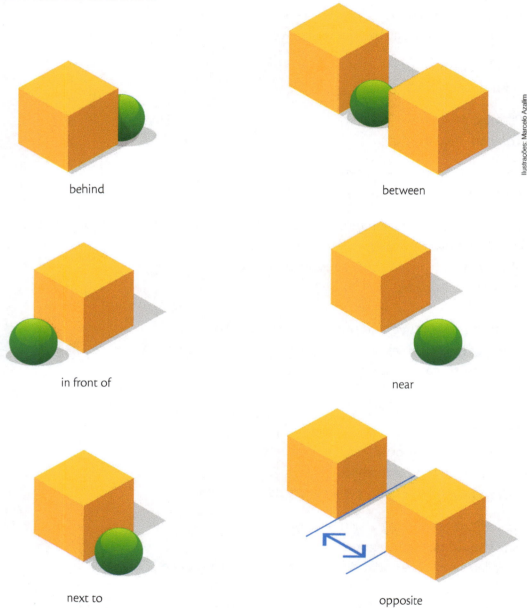

behind

between

in front of

near

next to

opposite

Page 58

There are some expressions that help people give directions.

turn right

turn left

go straight

||| Unit 5 |||

Page 73

The **past form** of the verb **to be** can be used to talk about facts that happened or were true at a certain moment in the past. Depending on the subject, it can be formed differently:

Pronoun	Affirmative	Negative	Interrogative
I	I was here.	I wasn't here.	Was I here?
You	You were here.	You weren't here.	Were you here?
He	He was here.	He wasn't here.	Was he here?
She	She was here.	She wasn't here.	Was she here?
It	It was here.	It wasn't here.	Was it here?
We	We were here.	We weren't here.	Were we here?
You	You were here.	You weren't here	Were you here?
They	They were here.	They weren't here.	Were they here?

Verb to be

Affirmative form	Negative form		Interrogative form
Full form	Full form	Short form	Full form
I was	I was not	I wasn't	Was I...?
He was She was It was	He was not She was not It was not	He wasn't She wasn't It wasn't	Was he...? Was she...? Was it...?
You were We were They were	You were not We were not They were not	You weren't We weren't They weren't	Were you...? Were we...? Were they...?

Examples

I was at school.	I was not (wasn't) at home.	Was I at home?
Daniel was in a hot-air balloon.	She was not (wasn't) on a bus.	Was he in a hot-air balloon?
Emma and Greg were friends.	They were not (weren't) brother and sister.	Were they friends?

Page 76 to 78

A **regular verb** is a verb that conforms to the rule for forming its **simple past tense** and past participle. The main rule is to add the suffix (-ed) or (-d) to the infinitive (base) form of the verb. However, depending on the last syllable of the verbs, this rule may suffer some adjustments. Look at the exceptions:

The verb ends in consonant – vowel – consonant (CVC)	The verb ends in consonant + (-y)	The verb ends in (-e)
double the final consonant + (**-ed**)	**take off the** (-y) **and add** (**-ied**)	**just add** (**-d**)
stop – stopped	cry – cried	like – liked
plan – planned	try – tried	believe – believed

The **simple past** is used to talk about facts that happened or were true at a certain moment in the past. The affirmative form of the past tense is formed by the **simple past form** of the verbs:
  I **listened** to the noise last night.
  She **stopped** by the restaurant on her way home.
  You **cried** a lot watching that movie last weekend.

To form the negative or the interrogative forms of the simple past, it is needed an **auxiliary verb** (**did**), and it comes before the **main verb in the base form**. To form negative sentences, add a negative (**not**) to the auxiliary verb:
  I **did not** (**didn't**) **listen** to the noise last night.
  She **did not** (**didn't**) **stop** by the restaurant on her way home.
  You **did not** (**didn't**) **cry** a lot watching that movie last weekend.

To form interrogative sentences, the **auxiliary verb** (**did**) comes at the beginning of the sentence, before the subject pronoun and the **main verb in the base form**.
  Did I **listen** to the noise last night?
  Did she **stop** by the restaurant on her way home?
  Did you **cry** a lot watching that movie last weekend?

||| Unit 6 |||

Page 90

Besides the verbs with regular past forms, there are others that are called **irregular verbs** as they do not follow a specific rule forming its **simple past** tense and **past participle**. Unfortunately, learning irregular verbs means memorization. Check the list with the irregular verb forms at the chart on pages 168, 169, 170 and 171. The affirmative, negative and interrogative forms of these verbs follow the same structure as the ones for the regular verbs.

The affirmative form of the past tense is formed by the **simple past form** of the verbs:
  I **bought** a present for you last night.
  She **forgot** her homework at home.
  You **went** to the movies last weekend.

To form the negative or the interrogative forms of the simple past, it is needed an **auxiliary verb** (did), and it comes before the **main verb in the base form**. To form negative sentences, add a negative (**not**) to the auxiliary verb:

I **did** **not** (**didn't**) **buy** a present for you last night.
She **did** **not** (**didn't**) **forget** her homework at home.
You **did** **not** (**didn't**) **go** to the movies last weekend.

To form interrogative sentences, the **auxiliary verb** (**did**) comes at the beginning of the sentence, before the subject pronoun and the **main verb in the base form**:

Did I **buy** a present for you last night?
Did she **forget** her homework at home?
Did you **go** to the movies last weekend?

||| Unit 7 |||

Page 104

Here is a set of words related to appearance traits.

Hair length	long medium short
Hair color	dark hair brown hair blond/blonde red hair dyed / stained hair gray hair brunet (man) brunette (woman)
Hair type	straight wavy curly afro bald
Weight	fat / chubby average slim/thin
Eyes	brown black green blue hazel
Other features	blind hunchbacked mustache beard dark circles wart wrinkles freckles pimples scar tattoos braces

Page 108

Here is a set of words related to personality traits.

Positive meaning		Negative meaning		Neutral
Brave	Cheerful	Absent-minded	Clumsy	Quiet
Honest	Easygoing	Coward	Dishonest	Noisy
Friendly	Generous	Disloyal	Disorganized	Old
Hard-working	Kind	Disrespectful	Foolish	Young
Loyal	Modest	Hesitant	Impatient	Sensitive
Neat	Optimistic	Jealous	Lazy	Shy
Organized	Patient	Mean	Pessimistic	
Polite	Reliable	Rude	Sad	
Respectful	Sensible	Selfish	Unfriendly	
Skillful	Trusting	Ungenerous	Unhesitant	
Tidy	Unselfish	Unreliable	Untidy	
Self-confident		Uptight		

Page 110

The expression **used to** is applied to refer or to talk about past habits, or things in the past that are no longer true. It can refer to repeated actions or to a state or situation. Look at its formation:

Affirmative	Negative	Interrogative
I used to be chubby.	I did not use to be chubby.	Did you use to be chubby?
She used to wear glasses.	She did not use to wear glasses.	Did she use to wear glasses?
They used to have freckles.	They did not use to have freckles.	Did they use to have freckles?

||| Unit 8 |||

Page 118

Here is a set of words related to climate and weather.

Hot Warm Sunny Clear	Cloudy Fog Haze Mist	Dew Wind Strong wind Hurricane
Cold Snow Snowflake Blizzard Frost Freeze	Rain Raindrop Hail Thunder Thunderstorm Lightening Overcast Drizzle Rain showers	Day Night Dawn Sunrise Dusk Sunset

Page 121 to 123

The **past continuous tense** is used to talk about what people were doing or what was happening when something else happened or at a specific time in the past (used when connected to the finished action).

Structure
Main verb: present participle, it means, the base form of the verb + (**-ing**).
Auxiliary verb: past tense of the verb **to be**: **was** or **were**.

- **Affirmative sentences**
Subject pronoun + auxiliary verb + present participle + complement.
I **was** read**ing**.
He / she / it **was** read**ing**.
We / you / they **were** read**ing**.

- **Negative sentences**
Subject pronoun + auxiliary verb + negative + present participle + complement

full form
I **was** not read**ing**.
He / she / it **was** not read**ing**.
We / you / they **were** not read**ing**.

short form
I **wasn't** read**ing**.
He / she / it **wasn't** read**ing**.
We / you / they **weren't** read**ing**.

- **Interrogative sentences**
Auxiliary verb + subject pronoun + present participle + complement?
Was I read**ing**?
Was he / she / it read**ing**?
Were we / you / they read**ing**?

The **present participle** is formed by adding (**-ing**) to the base form of the verbs. Pay attention to the rules:

Verb ending		Rule	
Consonant + (-e)	take	exchange (-e) by (-ing)	ta**king**
(-ie)	lie	exchange (-ie) by (-y) plus(-ing)	l**ying**
Vowel + consonant	put	double the last consonant plus (-ing)	put**ting**

IRREGULAR VERBS

BASE FORM OF VERB	SIMPLE PAST	PAST PARTICIPLE
be	was / were	been
beat	beat	beaten
become	became	become
begin	began	begun
bet	bet	bet
blow	blew	blown
break	broke	broken
bring	brought	brought
build	built	built
burst	burst	burst
buy	bought	bought
catch	caught	caught
choose	chose	chosen
come	came	come
cost	cost	cost
cut	cut	cut
deal	dealt	dealt
do	did	done
draw	drew	drawn
drink	drank	drunk
drive	drove	driven
eat	ate	eaten
fall	fell	fallen
feed	fed	fed
feel	felt	felt
fight	fought	fought
find	found	found

BASE FORM OF VERB	SIMPLE PAST	PAST PARTICIPLE
fly	flew	flown
forget	forgot	forgotten
freeze	froze	frozen
get	got	got / gotten
give	gave	given
go	went	gone
grow	grew	grown
hang	hung	hung
have	had	had
hear	heard	heard
hide	hid	hidden
hit	hit	hit
hold	held	held
hurt	hurt	hurt
keep	kept	kept
know	knew	known
lay	laid	laid
lead	led	led
leave	left	left
lend	lent	lent
let	let	let
lie	lay	lain
light	lit	lit
lose	lost	lost
make	made	made
mean	meant	meant
meet	met	met

BASE FORM OF VERB	SIMPLE PAST	PAST PARTICIPLE
pay	paid	paid
put	put	put
read	read	read
ride	rode	ridden
ring	rang	rung
rise	rose	risen
run	ran	run
say	said	said
see	saw	seen
sell	sold	sold
send	sent	sent
set	set	set
shake	shook	shaken
shine	shone	shone
shoot	shot	shot
show	showed	shown
shut	shut	shut
sing	sang	sung
sink	sank	sunk
sit	sat	sat
sleep	slept	slept
slide	slid	slid
speak	spoke	spoken
spend	spent	spent
spring	sprang	sprung
stand	stood	stood
steal	stole	stolen

BASE FORM OF VERB	SIMPLE PAST	PAST PARTICIPLE
stick	stuck	stuck
swear	swore	sworn
sweep	swept	swept
swim	swam	swum
swing	swung	swung
take	took	taken
teach	taught	taught
tear	tore	torn
tell	told	told
think	thought	thought
throw	threw	thrown
understand	understood	understood
wake	woke	woken
wear	wore	worn
weave	wove	woven
win	won	won
write	wrote	written

GLOSSARY

A

absent-minded: distraído; disperso
act: atuar; interpretar
action: ação
actually: realmente
adventure: aventura
affectionate: amoroso; carinhoso
agree: concordar
agreeableness: agradabilidade
ahead: em frente
allies: aliados
allow: permitir
alongside: ao lado de
amuse: divertir
animation: animação
answer: resposta
apple: maçã
asleep: adormecido
attire: traje
avocado: abacate

B

bacon: toucinho
back down: abandonar, desistir
bag: sacola; bolsa
bake: assar
bakery: padaria
bald: careca; calvo
bank: banco
beach: praia
beadwork: bordado de contas
beans: contas
beat down: brilhar intensamente
become: ser; tornar
beef: carne bovina
been missing: estar desaparecido
beg: pedir; implorar
begin: começar
behind: atrás
belie: desmentir
belong: pertencer
beloved: amado
belt: cinto; cinturão
bet: apostar
between: entre
biography: biografia
blazer: paletó
blond: loiro
blonde: pessoa loira
blood-related: consanguíneo
blouse: blusa
blow: soprar
blue: azul
boots: botas
bored: entediado
bossy: mandão, autoritário
boundaries: fronteiras
brave: corajoso; valente
bread: pão
bridge: ponte
broad: amplo
broccoli: brócolis
brown: marrom
brunet: moreno
brunette: morena
brush: escovar
building: prédio; construção
bus terminal: terminal de ônibus
butter: manteiga

C

cabbage: couve; repolho
cabinet: gabinete
cake: bolo
call: chamar; ligar
cap: boné
carrot: cenoura
cauliflower: couve-flor
change (someone's) mind: mudar de opinião
chaperone: acompanhante
cheerful: animado; contente
cheese: queijo
cherry: cereja
chicken: frango
childish: infantil
chocolate: chocolate
choose: escolher
chop: cortar em pequenos pedaços
chubby/fat: gordinho; gordo
church: igreja
cilantro: coentro
cinema: cinema
city hall: prefeitura
classical: clássica
clean: limpo
clear: claro
clerk: balconista, atendente.
climb up: escalar
cloth: tecido
clothes: roupa
cloudy: nublado
clumsy: desajeitado
coat: camada; casaco; agasalho
coffee: café
co-founders: cofundador
cold: frio
come (to come): chegar; vir
comedy: comédia
comfortable: confortável
commandeered: comandado
compass: bússola
conscientiousness: conscienciosidade
cook: cozinhar
cookie: bolacha; biscoito
cool: legal
corn: milho
countable: contável
country: país
covered: coberto

cry: chorar
cunning: astuta, hábil
cup: copo
curb: refrear
curly: encaracolado

D

dance: dançar
default: padrão
desire: desejar
detective: detetive
devices: dispositivos
dice: cortar em cubos
disagree: discordar
disagreeable: desagradável
discover: descobrir
discovery: descoberta
diseases: doenças
dishonest: desonesto
domineering: dominador
drama: drama
drap (to drap): drapejar
draw (to draw): desenhar
dress: vestido
dressing-room: camarim
drive: dirigir
drive out: sair
drizzle: garoa; chuviscar
drought: seca
drown: afogar
drums: percussão; bateria
dry (noun): seco
dry (verb): secar
dull: maçante; enfadonho

E

easy-going: fácil; pacato
egg: ovo
encounter: encontrar
entitled: intitulado
epic: épico
excited: excitado

exist: existir
extroversion: extroversão

F

face: enfrentar
fairy tale: conto de fadas
faithful: fiel; leal
fantasy: fantasia
fearful: medroso
fees: salários
fiction: ficção
fire department: brigada de incêndio
fish: peixe
fix: consertar
flip-flops: chinelos
fluffy: fofo
flute: flauta
foggy: nebuloso
folks: pessoas, povo
former: antigo
freedoms: liberdades
freezing: congelamento
fret: aborrecer-se
fridge: geladeira
frosty: frio; indiferente
fruit: fruta
funny: engraçado

G

gadgets: dispositivo
gain: ganhar
garlic: alho
garments: vestuário
gas station: posto de gasolina
gay: alegre
generally: geralmente
generous: generoso
get around: locomover-se
get dressed: vestir-se
glasses: óculos; copos
gloves: luvas

go: ir
go downhill: dar errado
go straight: ir direto/reto
go-to: rápida, ágil
goals: metas
goggled: esbugalhado
gown: vestimenta, vestido
grain: grão
grape: uva
grocery shop/store: quitanda
growth: crescimento
guilty: culpado
guitar: violão

H

ham: presunto
hamburger: hambúrguer
handle: lidar com
hands-on learning: aprendizagem prática
hang loose: descolado, desencanado, largado
happy: feliz
harm: prejudicar
harmful: prejudicial
hat: chapéu
hazel: avelã
headdress: touca
hearing-impaired: deficiente auditivo
heartbeat: batida do coração
heat (verb): esquentar
heat (noun): calor, aquecimento
hesitant: hesitante
high heels: salto alto
historical: histórico
horror: horror
hospital: hospital
hot: quente
hotel: hotel
hot-tempered: impetuoso, irritável

household: domicílio
humid: úmido
humor: humor
hungry: faminto

I

icy: gelado
illiterate: analfabeto
imaginative: imaginativo; criativo
immature: imaturo
imprison: aprisionar
in front of: diante de
insight: discernimento
inspire: inspirar

J

jacket: jaqueta
jam: geleia
jazz: jazz
jealous: ciumento
jeans: jeans; calças
join: juntar
joyful: alegre
juice: suco
jumper: agasalho

K

key: chave
kind: gentil
kinesthetic: cinestésico
kite: pipa
know: saber

L

label (noun): rótulo
label (verb): nomear, rotular
lazy: preguiçoso
lead: conduzir
learn: aprender

leave: deixar; partir
left (noun): esquerda
left (verb): deixar
legend: legenda
length: comprimento
lettuce: alface
library: biblioteca
lime: limão
literate: alfabetizado
locked into: estar preso
long-buried: há muito enterrado
long-lost: perdido há muito tempo
long run: long prazo
loyal: leal, fiel

M

make: fazer
mall: alameda; shopping center
medium heat: fogo médio
meat: carne
milk: leite
mix: mexer
modern: moderno
movies: cinema
museum: museu
mustard: mostarda

N

near: próximo; perto
neat: limpo; puro
neuroticism: neuroticismo
news: notícia
next to: ao lado de; perto de
nodd: acenar com a cabeça
noisy: barulhento
nonprofit organization: organização não governamental
noodles: talharim
nuts: castanha

O

oat: aveia
obtain: obter
oddbal: excêntrico
old: velho
olive oil: azeite
one-upping: superar, ser melhor do que alguém
onion: cebola
onwards: em diante
openness: abertura
opposite to: contrário/oposto a
optimistic: otimista
orange: laranja
ostensibly: ostensivamente
out loud: em voz alta
over and over: repetidamente

P

pajamas: pijama
pants: calça
papaya: mamão
park: parque
parking lot: estacionamento
partially cloud: parcialmente nublado
pasta: massa; macarrão
pear: pera
pepper: pimenta
piano: piano
pie: torta
pineapple: abacaxi
pipe: gaita (de foles)
pitch: tom
place: colocar
play: tocar um instrumento; brincar, jogar
pleasing: agradável
plunge: mergulhar
poetry: poesia
police station: delegacia
polite: educado

174

polluted: poluído
pop: estilo musical pop
post office: correios
potato: batata
poverty: pobreza
pregnant: grávida
protein: proteína
psychokinetic: telecinético
purse: bolsa; carteira
put on: colocar
put on trial: colocado em julgamento
puzzles: quebra-cabeças

Q

quest: busca
quiet: quieta; calma
quirky: peculiar

R

rain: chuva
raincoat: capa de chuva
rainy: chuvoso
rap: estilo musical rap
rate: classificar, avaliar
reach (to reach): alcançar
recipe: receita
red: vermelho
reggae: estilo musical reggae
regret: arrepender-se
rehearse: ensaiar
reliable: confiável
remaining: que sobraram
restaurant: restaurante
rice: arroz
ride: viagem
right: certo
rock: estilo musical rock
romance: romance
rubbish: lixo
run: correr

S

sad: triste
samba: estilo musical samba
sandwich: sanduíche
sausage: salsicha
sax/saxophone: saxofone
scarf: cachecol
school: escola
sci-fi: ficção científica
season: temperar
seem: parecer
seek: procurar
selfish: egoísta
set: configurar; estabelecer
several: vários
sew: costurar
sharp: aguçada; afiada
shirt: camisa
shine: brilho
shoes: sapatos
shop: loja
short (adjective): curto; pequeno
shorts (noun): short (peça de roupa)
silk: seda
simmer: cozinhar lentamente
sing: cantar
ski: esquiar
skirt: saia (peça de roupa)
slavery: escravidão
slim: magro; esbelto
smart: esperto
sneakers: tênis
snow: neve
snowy: nevado
socks: meias
span: abranger
spend: gastar
spit out: cuspir
sports center: centro esportivo
spotlight: holofote, local de destaque
start: iniciar; começar
steak: bife; filé
steal: roubar
stop: parar; terminar
store: loja
stormy: tempestuoso
strawberry: morango
subway: metrô
suit: terno
sunglasses: óculos de sol
sunny: ensolarado
sunrise: nascer do sol
sunset: pôr do sol
supermarket: supermercado
sustainable: sustentável
sweater: suéter; agasalho
sweet-potato: batata doce
swim: nadar
swindlers: vigaristas, trapaceiros
syrup: calda

T

tactile: tátil
take: tomar; pegar
take away: levar embora; tomar
take off: desgrudar; tirar
tall: alto
tbsp (tablespoon): colher de sopa
tea: chá
tender: sensível, delicado
theater: teatro
thin: magro
threat: ameaçar
thriller: filme de suspense
tidy: arrumar
tie: amarrar; prender
tight-knit: unidos
take a stand: se posicionar, fazer uma escolha
thunder: trovão
track down: rastrear
toasted: torrado

tomato: tomate
tomboy: menina que apresenta um estilo tradicionalmente associado a meninos
tools: ferramentas
traffic: trânsito
trouble: problema
trousers: calça comprida
try on: provar roupa
t-shirt: camiseta
turkey: peru
turn: virar
twin: gêmeo
two-third: dois terços

U

umbrella: guarda-chuva
unaware: inconsciente, sem saber
uncountable: incontável
uncover: descobrir
underground: metrô
unearths: desenterrar
unfit: impróprio

unimaginative: sem imaginação
unloving: desprovido de afeto
unpredictable: imprevisível
unreliable: não confiável
untidy: sujo, desarrumado
upset: chateado; aborrecido

V

vegetables: vegetais; legumes
violin: violino

W

wallet: carteira
warm: quente
wart: verruga
wasp: vespa
watch: assistir
water: água
watermelon: melancia
wear: usar; vestir
wearer: portador.
weave: tecer

weavers: tecelões
weasel out of: escapar ou evitar algo
well dressed: bem vestido
well-known: bem conhecido
wet: molhado
windy: ventoso
winter: inverno
wise: sábio
within: dentro
wreck: naufragar, afundar
wristwatch: relógio de pulso

X

Y

yogurt: iogurte
young: jovem

Z

zucchini: abobrinha